Peak  Every Time

Peak performances should not be left to chance. Rather than hoping that you will perform at your best, why not engineer your performance?

Peak Performance Every Time incorporates principles from sport psychology and performance coaching and applies these to all areas of life, with a particular focus on business. Using illustrations and real-world examples from top athletes and business executives, it focuses on the three main components that underpin performance:

- Confidence
- Motivation
- Focus.

As well as offering practical strategies to help the reader achieve their optimal mindset, it also explains how to coach others to perform to their potential. Throughout, the book is underpinned by theoretical frameworks, literature and research findings and will be invaluable to anyone trying to reach their full potential, in particular athletes, coaches, managers and executives. It will also be of interest to sports psychology, management and business students.

Simon Hartley is an experienced sport psychologist and performance coach. During the last 15 years, he has worked with British Olympians, world record holders and championship winning teams, and at the highest level of sport, including spells in Premier League football, Premiership rugby union and first-class county cricket. Since 2005, Simon has also applied the principles of sport psychology to business, education and the charity sector.

Peak Performance Every Time

Simon Hartley

Routledge
Taylor & Francis Group

LONDON AND NEW YORK

First published 2012
by Routledge
27 Church Road, Hove, East Sussex BN3 2FA

Simultaneously published in the USA and Canada
by Routledge
711 Third Avenue, New York NY 10017

*Routledge is an imprint of the Taylor & Francis Group,
an Informa business*

© 2012 Psychology Press

British Library Cataloguing in Publication Data
A catalogue record for this book is available from the British Library

Library of Congress Cataloging in Publication Data
Hartley, Simon.
  Peak performance every time / Simon Hartley.
     p. cm.
  Includes bibliographical references and index.
  ISBN 978-0-415-67673-1 (hbk) – ISBN 978-0-415-67674-8 (pbk)
1. Success. 2. Success in business. 3. Performance–Psychological
aspects. 4. Self-management (Psychology) I. Title.
  BF637.S8H333 2012
  158.1–dc23
                    2011027171

                         ISBN: 978–0–415–67673–1 (hbk)
                         ISBN: 978–0–415–67674–8 (pbk)
                         ISBN: 978–0–203–14166–3 (ebk)

                    Typeset in New Century Schoolbook by
                    Garfield Morgan, Swansea, West Glamorgan

Contents

Foreword

It was in the Lake District on a climbing and outdoor activities week that I first came across Simon Hartley more than 15 years ago. He was asked to lead a group on the hills in tough conditions where the mist meant it was hard to see more than a few metres in front at times. The experienced mountaineer who was in charge had asked Simon to navigate our way off the summit. Simon, like the rest of the party, had little experience or knowledge of mountain craft so this was quite a shock to him. We survived and he did a good job, but was less than pleased at being put in this situation. Later that night, as the group representative, he approached the mountain leaders to ask why he was allowed to do something for which he felt so very unprepared. I watched as he asked his questions and saw that he did not like the answers! This book is a continuation of that journey he started all those years ago.

Having the courage to ask questions is always a good thing. When those questions are about yourself, it is usually something both harder to do and yet often more worthwhile. This is really how all authentic learning takes place – it is always personal, which is maybe why so many seem to do all they can to avoid this. Learning demands that we become ready to learn. This means that we may need to accept our ignorance and empty ourselves of our unexamined ideas. To learn, really learn, means that we have to give our whole selves over to the task – no half measures. This can be quite scary at times, especially when we don't know what to expect or don't like what we find out.

Although this book is meant to be about performance, I like to think that it is really about learning as well. The message running throughout is that to perform every time we must be ready to start again and again. Sometimes this is from a new place, but often it is harder than this because it is from a place that is familiar to us! Letting go is not easy, but not to let go is never to learn.

Like the answers Simon got that day in the hills and from the many experiences he has had since then in his professional and personal life, sometimes new ideas cause us to feel uncertain and even uncomfortable. They can shake our long-held beliefs and make us feel uneasy. Fortunately, they are also very exciting! When we start to learn and perform better we want more and more. Sometimes we find that this can only be had by having less and less. Our world and outlook can be turned on its head – all very exhilarating and enlivening. But, and this is so important, this book does not let us imagine that this can usually be achieved easily. Words like responsibility, courage and anxiety used in this work give a welcome reality check to what we sometimes can hear elsewhere. We live in times when a quick-fix culture is running rampant. This can be seen in relationships between people, in business and politics, and even in education, psychology and medicine. 'I want now' has appeared to have swamped 'I need later'. This book is counter-cultural in reminding us of the truth that the best of things rarely come easily to us. It also challenges the equally flawed notion that achievement is to be found in the worship of effort and the cult of over-exertion and busyness.

The themes that Simon relies upon have emerged from a wide range of individuals and different performance environments. This is a great strength of the book. Inspiration from these stories is the best way to stimulate people to want to know more. To this end the final chapter is a refreshingly broad and yet deep account of other literature that will answer more questions on this journey. Accounts from sport, business, science and other areas of human performance are underpinned by theory and practice.

There is much here to inspire when needed (always) and to give direction where we lose our way (often). I commend this book to you and hope it will be something that is read in the manner advocated by Dr Johnson: 'read just as inclination leads him: for what he reads as a task will do him little good'.

Mark Nesti
Reader in Sport Psychology
Liverpool John Moores University, UK

Preface

I am incredibly fortunate to have worked in the fields of elite sport and sport psychology for the last 15 years or so. As an undergraduate sport science student, I had the opportunity of working in professional and international sport. This gave me a fantastic introduction to life as a practitioner. When I started, I did what most people do. I began by trying to apply the knowledge that I had learned in the classroom. I took the textbook theories and the research into the field.

Of course, I had limited success initially. Gradually, over the course of the next 15 years or so, I refined my approaches. Experiences give us opportunities to learn. They help us to understand how effective some strategies are and how limited others are. Over the years, I built on the methods that were effective and started to steer away from those that weren't working for me. In practice, there is a simple, hard truth. What you do *has* to work! It has to make a positive impact. It has to achieve the desired result. Therefore, the tools that I put in my tool box were the ones I could rely on to get the best possible results quickly, effectively and consistently. At the highest level of sport there is little margin for error. My experiences in Premiership football, Premiership rugby union, Super League (rugby league), Olympic sports, golf, tennis and motor sport all emphasize the critical importance of using strategies that work. The reality is that there is often a hair's breadth between winning and losing, but the difference in the rewards can be astronomical.

Obviously, this is not just true of elite sport. It is also true in business and many other realms of life. Around five years ago, a sales manager approached me and asked if I could help his team. It was the turn of the year and the team's target had increased by 50 per cent from the previous year. Interestingly, the team had only just scraped through in the previous year. The sales manager had a problem. He didn't believe the team could achieve the new target and neither did they. I'd never worked with a sales team before, so I decided simply to view the team as a group of athletes and apply my tried and tested sport psychology strategies. To my surprise, they worked extremely well. The team became confident, motivated and focused. As a result, they exceeded their targets.

Initially it took me a while to understand why it had worked so well. I was puzzled as to how sport psychology applied so easily to a business environment. The answer of course is very simple. There is a simple common denominator. We are all humans. Once I'd realized this, I began to apply the same principles to many other fields, including executive coaching, leadership and management development, performance management, other sales teams, education and the charity sector. Consequently, I have also learned to draw on methods that lie outside of sport psychology. Some of the approaches I now use with athletes come from business environments, education and mainstream psychology. I have included the references so that you can explore some of these incredibly valuable resources for yourself. The final chapter of the book identifies some of the theory and research that underpins these methods.

This book explains how to apply performance coaching strategies to your life. To help the ideas come to life, I've used some live examples from my work with athletes, sports teams, executives and business organizations. I genuinely hope that you find these as useful as I have, and that they have a positive impact on your performance and your life.

Acknowledgements

Thank you to my wonderful wife, my beautiful girls, my incredibly supportive parents and my fantastic family.

Thank you to my friends, who also provide constant support. In particular, I would like to thank Dean Riddle, Mark Nesti, Paul Laver, Dave Hompes, Chris Cook and Justin Perkins, whose friendship and help have been unwavering.

I would also like to thank Mihaly Csikszentmihalyi for his kind permission to use his challenge and skills model within this book (see Figure 3.1).

Introduction

Your performance is entirely within your control. Your performance is not dictated by anyone else or anything else. It's not dictated by circumstances or external factors. Your performance emanates from your thoughts and your feelings. Nobody can influence your thoughts or feelings, unless you let them! No situation or circumstance can impact on your thoughts or feelings, unless you allow it (Manz, 2000).

You have ultimate control over how you think and feel. Therefore, you have ultimate control over your performance: 'Between stimulus and response is our greatest power – the power to choose' (Covey, 2004). So why is it that many people's performances are so inconsistent? Even elite athletes often struggle to control their mindset and emotions. Many elite athletes are affected by external influences and other people. The fact is we all have the power to control our mind and emotions. However, most people give their power away.

I have recently started working with a squad of elite junior fencers. The director of fencing initially approached me because the athletes were displaying a great deal of frustration and anger on the piste (the piste is the fencing equivalent of a pitch or a court; it is the narrow strip that they compete on). The problem is that if they display their frustration during competition, they risk being 'black carded' (disqualified) and banned from the competition for several months.

I started by talking with the fencers about the things that made them frustrated. They listed a host of factors that affected them. One athlete said that when the opponent celebrates, it really winds him up. Another said that if he was fighting an opponent who he was 'supposed to beat easily', he would get really frustrated when they scored a point against him. Others were affected by the referee, the opponent's supporters or the opponent's trash talk. At the end of the discussion, I asked them who had control over their mindset and their emotions. It was obvious that the fencers had given control of their own thoughts and feelings to just about everyone else. As a result, they were being ruled by other people and by circumstance. They had strapped themselves into a mental and emotional rollercoaster because they had given up control. Job number one for the fencers is to start taking control back. We have control until we give it over to someone else or something else.

Through the course of this book I will show you how to engineer the three key elements of your mental game. We will discover how to:

- control confidence;
- master motivation;
- hone focus.

I will help you to take control over your mind and your emotions, and therefore help you to engineer your performance. Your performance should not be left to chance. Many people's performance is subject to a host of variables. Too many people say 'I hope I'll do okay today'. I'd argue that hoping is not enough. Wouldn't you rather *know* that you're going to perform well? Wouldn't you rather *know* that you have the ability to control your mind and your emotions? If you have control of your thoughts and feelings, you have a very good chance of producing a peak performance.

Most athletes, and indeed most people, would say that their aim is to win. I speak to many athletes who tell me that they're happy if they win and disappointed if they lose. The same is often true in business. We have targets and goals to achieve, and we are focused on hitting them. However, the reality is usually different. In both sport and business, often there can only be one winner. So, most people actually tend to set themselves a different stall. Many people actually are satisfied if they have performed to their potential and are disappointed if they drop short. Genuine World Class performers in any discipline are normally dissatisfied with a below-par performance even if they do win. Although no-one likes losing, they will often be satisfied if they lost but produced their very best performance on the day. If this is true for most of us, then our true aim is probably to achieve our potential and produce our peak performance:

> When I go out and race, I'm not trying to beat opponents, I'm trying to beat what I have done . . . to beat myself, basically. People find that hard to believe because we've had such a bias to always strive to win things. If you win something and you haven't put everything into it, you haven't actually achieved anything at all. When you've had to work hard for something and you've got the best you can out of yourself on that given day, that's where you get satisfaction from.
>
> (Ian Thorpe, Australian Olympic Swimmer)

As a sport psychologist and performance coach, this is my aim. People often ask me how I help to boost people's performances. I guess many people imagine that I magically inject them with some kind of mental rocket fuel. Some people imagine that I hypnotize people to give them super-human abilities. Obviously neither of these is true. I often explain to people that my job does not involve magic wands. I do not have any mental rocket packs. My job is not to give a performer anything they don't already have. In a sense, my role is not to enhance anything. Instead, my job is to take away the things that stop you from producing your potential: Performance = Potential − Interference (Gallwey, 1986).

As a performance coach, my job is to reduce the interference as much as possible. Instead of strapping a mental rocket pack to you, maybe the aim is simply to release the hand brake. Most people think that the best way to make a car go quicker would be to push the throttle harder. Maybe the best way is to make sure that you've released the brakes fully first.

This interference, or baggage as it's sometimes called, comes from all sorts of sources. One of the most common sources is fear. Fear of failure. Fear of success. Fear of letting someone else down. Fear of looking daft. Fear of what other people will think of you if you screw up. Many people's performance is actually affected by a host of outside issues and agendas that they bring into play. In reality, our mental agendas have nothing whatsoever to do with the actual performance, but we allow them in and invite them to affect our mind and emotions.

Throughout the following chapters, we will also look at where this interference comes from and how to minimize it. We will examine the sources and how to change our mindset to reduce their impact on us. We will look at how we actually create much of this interference, and therefore how we can dismantle it.

During a recent conversation, a martial artist told me that he was feeling pressure to live up to everyone else's expectations. He felt the need to show the people around him that he was good at his sport and that he could be a champion. As we discussed it further, the athlete told me how he'd been bullied for a long time as a child and young adult. As a result, he had a real desire to prove himself to everyone else and show them how successful he was. This all acts as baggage. In reality, this agenda has nothing to do with his fight. It has nothing to do with the moves he has to make, how he counters the opponent's moves or how he executes his technique. Instead, it acts as baggage, pulling his focus away from the important things that will allow him to perform. Instead of focusing on what he needs to do to perform well, he worries about what will happen if he doesn't perform well. The techniques and strategies in this book are here to help you to *just do it*.

When there is too much interference, we often get caught up in a negative spiral. When we make a mistake, we tend to get frustrated. As this happens, we often start to over-analyze and over-think our performance (Gallwey, 1986; Flegal and Anderson, 2008). We may experience this as a phenomenon called 'trying too hard'. The likelihood is that when we try too hard and over-think, we will make another mistake. This then fuels the spiral of deteriorating performance. Spirals such as these have been researched in management (Lindsley, Brass and Thomas, 1995). Sport psychologist Thelma Horn (2008) has also applied 'confidence–performance spirals' to sport. In this book, we will identify ways to break this cycle and turn it into a positive, confident spiral. This can only be done if you are in control. Control is the vital ingredient.

So where do we start? How do you start taking control over your mind and emotions? What's the first step? Fundamentally, you need to have two things:

1 *Awareness*. You need to know yourself and understand yourself. You need to know how your mind and emotions tend to work. We're all different and there is no blueprint to work from. However, we can all learn

about our mental and emotional patterns simply by reflecting on what we do, what we say, how we think and how we feel (Wan, 2009; Hatzimoysis, 2010).

2 *Responsibility.* We need to take responsibility for our thoughts and feelings. Once we take responsibility, we stop blaming other people or circumstances for how we feel (Jauncey, 2002). We need to recognize that if someone says something that makes us feel angry, scared, upset or uncomfortable, we have allowed that person to control our emotions. We gave control to them. We ultimately have the ability to control how we feel. Therefore, it is not the other person's fault we feel bad, it is our responsibility to take control. There is a strong relationship between responsibility and control (Martin Fischer and Ravizza, 1998; Koestenbaum and Block, 2001; Nesti, 2004). When we take responsibility, we can take control.

As with everything, it's always easier said than done. Changing your mindset and taking control of your thoughts and emotions are not things that you can do at the click of your fingers. These are things that need to be learned. Normally, learning takes time. Inevitably, it requires us to make mistakes. As human beings we learn everything in the same way we learned to walk. We use the same basic tools and go through the same processes (Gallwey, 1986; Cook, 2005).

If you've ever watched babies learn to walk you will notice that they all fall over. In fact, they fall over a lot. Falling over is essential. Without falling over, they would not learn to walk. Babies are incredibly smart learners. For a start, you'll notice that they very rarely fall over the same way twice. That is because they constantly refine what they do and try it slightly differently each time.

I'd recommend banning the phrase 'If at first you don't succeed, try, try again' and replacing it with this: 'If at first you don't succeed, change and try again . . . then change it and try again'. If we follow this simple formula we will eventually succeed. As adults we often don't follow such a formula. Instead, we get upset if we try three or four times and fail. If we fail enough times we give up. Babies have no concept of failure. To them, falling over is not failure. Because of this, babies don't reach a point where they consider giving up. Instead, they keep trying, changing and trying again until they get it right. We still have that incredible ability to learn. The only thing standing in our way is our perception of failure.

Imagine if Humphry Davy, Joseph Wilson-Swan and Thomas Edison had given up when inventing the light bulb? What if they had tried a dozen times without success and decided to give up? What if they had become despondent after 100 failed trials, or 1000? Edison trialled thousands of different materials for his filament before he had a commercially viable light bulb.

'A journey of 1000 miles starts with a single step' (Anon). In fact, a journey of 1000 miles is entirely composed of single steps. If you can take one step, then simply repeat that step many times and you can walk 1000 miles. Taking control of your mind and emotions is a step-by-step process. It is a journey that can only be walked one step at a time. Your path towards engineering your peak performance consistently is a series of very manageable single steps. Like the journey of 1000 miles, it takes time and perseverance. Everyone is capable of making the journey as long as they keep taking the steps and learning the way they learned as a baby.

Summary

- You have ultimate control over your thoughts and your emotions.
- Only you can give that control away.
- When we take responsibility, we take control.
- Understanding ourselves is vital.
- It all takes time and requires mistakes. When learning to walk we must expect to fall over.

1

Experiencing peak performance

Peak performances and peak experiences are often described using a number of different terms. You will often hear people refer to *The Zone* or a *Flow State*. Essentially these terms refer to the same phenomenon. They describe a state of complete concentration and total absorption. People often report that peak performances seem effortless. They seem to have more time, see things more clearly and find the performance easy. Some have described feeling like they have a Midas touch. Everything they seem to attempt comes off (Jackson and Csikszentmihalyi, 1999).

Research into *The Zone* tells us that there are a number of consistent features. *The Zone* is a state in which we are completely involved in an activity for its own sake. We lose ourselves in the task. We become immersed. Simply doing the activity becomes its own reward. Psychologists call this *optimal intrinsic motivation*, which refers to a state where our whole being is involved in the task. We are so focused on the activity that we have almost no way of being distracted. There is no spare attention for anything else. In fact, there is probably not enough attention to even focus on ourselves (Jackson and Csikszentmihalyi, 1999).

It is noticeable that many accounts of peak performances talk about people becoming 'at one with the task'. In essence, their sense of self seems to recede. Their ego steps back into the shadows and they lose themselves in the activity. This often leads people to lose track of time. They report that hours seem like minutes. This is illustrated by an account of a composer:

> That timelessness aspect of flow is so true! When I compose, I sometimes sit at the piano for over 4 hours without realizing a moment has gone by! It used to be that way with practicing other composers' work, but that lost a bit of its 'flow' magic after 15 years or so! It truly is one of the weirdest and most rewarding feelings in the world out there!
>
> (Pureakero, 2008)

Many people also describe a performance where every action, movement and thought flows inevitably from the previous one. It is a heightened state of consciousness where attention is extremely focused. It has been described as the state of mind where attention and motivation meet:

> A special place where performance is exceptionally consistent, automatic and flowing. An athlete is able to let his or her body deliver the performance it has learned so well.
>
> (Murphy, 1996: 4)

As you can imagine, accounts like these might be expected from elite athletes. However, peak performances are a feature of any walk of life. There are many reports from surgeons, artists and musicians. Mihaly Csikszentmihalyi, the principal researcher of flow states and peak experiences, has conducted over 8000 interviews with those who have experienced being *in flow*. His interviews cross occupations, demographic groups and cultures. They include accounts from Dominican monks, blind nuns, Himalayan climbers and Navaho shepherds.

Here are a few accounts given by people describing their experience of being *in flow*. They are taken from a Keynote presentation that Mihaly Csikszentmihalyi delivered to a

Technology Education Design Conference on 24 October 2008:

Music composer
You are in an ecstatic state to such a point that you feel as though you almost don't exist. I have experienced this time and again. My hand seems devoid of myself, and I have nothing to do with what's happening. I just sit there watching it in a state of awe and wonderment. And the music just flows out of itself.

Poet
It's like opening a door that's floating in the middle of nowhere and all you have to do is go and turn the handle, and open it and let yourself sink into it. You can't particularly force yourself into it. You just have to float. If there is any gravitational pull, it is from the outside world trying to keep you back from the door.

Figure skater
It was just one of those programs that clicked. I mean, everything just went right, everything felt good . . . it's just such a rush, like you feel it could go on and on and on, like you don't want it to stop because it's going so well. It's like you don't have to think, it's like everything goes automatically without thinking . . . it's like you're on autopilot so you don't have any thoughts. You hear the music but you're not aware that you're hearing it, because it's a part of it all.

Bob Beamon reported such a heightened state of concentration during his world record long jump of 29 feet and 2½ inches at the 1968 summer Olympics in Mexico City. It was more than 2 feet farther than the previous world record, and the record stood for over 20 years until Mike Powell broke it in 1991. Looking back and trying to explain his 1968 jump, Beamon described it in this way:

There is no answer for the performance. But everything was just perfect for it, the runway, my takeoff—I went six feet in the air when usually I'd go about five—and my concentration was perfect. It never happened quite that way before. I blocked out everything in the world, except my focus on the jump.

(Berkow, 1984: 289)

Although we've looked at examples from specific disciplines, peak performances are not limited to any particular fields. You have the potential to experience peak performances in almost anything you do. During your life, you will have experienced moments where you've been 'in the zone'. You may have been writing something, cooking, negotiating a deal, doing a presentation or building some DIY furniture. The task is irrelevant. Even some apparently mundane tasks can provide people with peak experiences. Mihaly Csikszentmihalyi (2008) gives an example of a man whose job it is to slice fish. Slicing fish may not seem like a particularly engaging task. However, he dedicates his professional life to slicing his fish perfectly. He constantly pushes himself to perfect his technique and ensure that he slices evenly and consistently, following the striations on the flesh. The chef sees his job as an art form, similar to that of a sculptor.

I have used this same principle when working with a café restaurant chain. Most people waiting tables or serving food in a busy café wouldn't necessarily focus on achieving a peak performance. Many of the roles would probably be viewed as unskilled or menial. Most waiting staff probably start their shift with the primary aim of getting through it and going home as quickly as possible. However, we sought to adopt a different tack. As the song says, 'It's not what you do, it's the way that you do it'.

I discovered that there are a lot of skilled roles in a café. Making a coffee is a prime example. There are around a dozen steps to making a perfect espresso shot, all of which have to be executed exceptionally well in order to produce a great coffee. In addition, for a latté or cappuccino, there is a great deal of skill required to get the milk to the optimal consistency and texture. No wonder there is a World Championship for Baristas.

Our job was not to make coffee. Our job was to make truly great coffee, and to take pride in the quality of coffee that we produced. We had internal competitions for our Baristas and sent them on training courses to teach them how to make even better coffee. The same was true of baking bread, preparing smoothies and juices, serving customers, cooking and presenting food and even wiping down tables. How many tables have you seen in restaurants that aren't quite clean? How many servers have you seen wiping crumbs onto the floor or onto a chair? It seems like a very simple task and yet few people manage to execute it consistently well in the middle of a manic Saturday lunchtime shift. As with most things, it is easy to do the job poorly. It's both more challenging and more rewarding when we do the job really well.

By this point in the chapter you will no doubt have noticed a number of recurring themes. Peak performances tend to occur when there are a number of key ingredients present. The first is clear focus. It is very hard to have complete concentration on something if you don't have a clear focus. In *flow states*, action and awareness merge when there is total immersion in the task. This immersion is only possible when you have a genuine love for what you do and are happy to throw yourself into it, lock, stock and barrel. Focus follows interest (Gallwey, 2003). In order to be 100 per cent focused on an activity, you have to want to do it purely for its own sake.

In order for many of the other ingredients to fall into place, you will need to be confident, excited, energized and in a pretty good mood. However, there are two other elements that are necessary for a person to truly achieve a peak performance. There needs to be a balance between the challenge presented and the skills of the individual. More specifically, there needs to be a balance between the challenge that the individual perceives and the level of skill that they believe they have. When we have a level of challenge that really pushes us, and the skills to be able to display mastery, we stand a very good chance of performing to our potential. We need to be stretched to the limits of our capacity, but we also need to be confident that we have the ability to master the task. If we have the challenge but not the belief in our skills, we will experience anxiety. If we have the skills but we don't perceive that it is a stimulating challenge, we will become bored (Jackson and Csikszentmihalyi, 1999) (see Figure 3.1 on page 46).

In the café restaurant business, we sought to increase the level of challenge by continually raising the standards and asking for greater and greater attention to detail. Where we asked people to engage in tasks that they were unfamiliar with, we made sure that they learned the skills fully. This ensured that they were confident in their ability and knew that they could deliver the standards that we expected. Many athletes I work with describe this as having 'trust' in their skills (Gallwey, 1986). When they trust, they are able to operate in that mindless state where they think less, stop trying and *just do it*.

The examples from the café business are typical of everyday life. We're not all composers, poets or elite athletes. Nonetheless, we have the opportunity to excel in what we do. You will have probably experienced peak performances in your life and may have surprised yourself with something that you did. It might have been whilst playing sport, working or engaged in a hobby. You may have regular and prolonged experiences of peak performances, or they may have been only fleeting glimpses.

Think back to peak moments. Have you been doing a task and become completely absorbed in it to the point where you lose track of time? Did you start to feel as if everything started to flow and almost became automatic? Did you do things so well that you surprised yourself? Did you do things you didn't realize you could do or that you'd not planned to do? If you've experienced some of these, you would probably describe it as a peak performance.

The performances and experiences that we've described so far are considerably different from most people's norm. Ordinarily, performances can be tinged with frustration. Things don't quite come off as you'd hoped. The performance is not exactly effortless and flowing. Instead, we experience interference. We question, we doubt, we over-think and over-analyze. We become overly aware of our thoughts and our frustrations (Nideffer, 2007). It's a far cry from losing ourselves in our activity. In contrast we seem to be connected to the activity very loosely, by a very thin thread. In fact, our connection often breaks, we force ourselves to re-connect, then it breaks again, and so on. The whole process gets a little bogged down, laborious and fragmented (Flegal and Anderson, 2008).

Through the course of the following ten chapters we will look at how we can control our internal environment to allow ourselves to experience peak performances consistently and regularly. The environment we create will allow us to either flourish or struggle. Imagine a garden that is enclosed indoors. If you create an ideal climate, life will flourish. If the environment is too hot, too cold, too dry or too wet, life will struggle. We will look at the fundamental conditions that allow peak performances to flourish and how you can control them. In the following chapters we will look primarily at how to control focus, confidence and motivation. We will also look at how to control the interferences that normally prevent people from experiencing a peak performance, such as fear and pressure.

Experience tells me that there are very few techniques, or skills, that can be directly applied to controlling thoughts and emotions (Corlett, 1996). Instead, there are many underlying factors that need to be addressed in order for us to have genuine control. Many people would advocate using techniques such as imagery. However, being able to imagine success tends to have very little impact on a person who is extremely scared about a performance (Nesti, 2004). Positive thinking probably won't have a significant impact either. There is normally a reason why the person is so scared. Sometimes, we have to dig a little deeper to actually address these issues and truly change our thoughts and feelings (Nesti, 2004). Fundamentally, we have to know who we are (Frankl, 1959/1984). We have to know ourselves and be happy with ourselves (Seligman, 2005). We have to be comfortable in our own skin and with our lives if we are going to truly lose ourselves in an activity (Csikszentmihalyi, 1990). We need to be happy to step away from the ego that most of us rely upon to present a front to the world. Our ego is the part of us that projects our outward image. We use the ego to give the world an impression of who we want to be. For many people, that impression may not be consistent with who we believe we are (Metzinger, 2010). Our ego wants to show the world how successful we are, even though we might be broke. Our ego wants the world to think we look good, even though we might believe we're ugly, or fat or miss-shapen. So, it's not always easy for us to abandon our ego, lose our self-consciousness and leap headlong into an activity especially if:

- someone is watching us;
- the outcome is important to us and the task is something we identify ourselves with;
- we care about what other people think.

A few years ago I was asked to work with a Super League (rugby league) player. This particular player was the star of his team. He was their highest paid player and their big name. Unfortunately he was experiencing a poor run of form. He was making mistake after mistake and his confidence was eroding fast. Here is a short piece from one of the session summaries I sent him:

> As we finished up the session, we started talking about the bigger issues that tend to be the real cause. You mentioned that rugby was really important to you (close to life and death importance). Although it's great to care about your game and although it's important to be a good pro, the flip side of the coin is that we can care too much. If rugby is your life and rugby is not going well, it affects everything. It means that your life will not go well. That's actually quite a fragile place to be. The big work that we need to do is to make sure that rugby is just a *part* of your life, and that there is plenty of other important stuff in there as well. You are not just a rugby player. As a person, you are far more than that. Sometimes we all forget that we are more than our job. Many players will just see themselves as an athlete and forget the rest. If you can be happy with you, and happy with life, you're in a stronger position. If you have a dip in form or make mistakes, you are much more likely to just let it go. It doesn't make you any less of a professional because you will always work hard on your game. It simply makes you a more rounded and balanced individual.
>
> Have fun at the weekend because that's what it's all about. If it's not enjoyable, we ought to ditch it and find something that is fun. To be fair, there can't be many things more enjoyable than playing rugby for a living.

Similar issues emerged when I worked with an elite junior squash player who was struggling to play her best game in the big competitions:

> We started by chatting about how you began playing squash. You mentioned that your Dad was a pro and

that you started by just playing around with a racket when you were about six years old. It sounds like squash was just something you did for fun because you were around the club a lot. When you were 12 years old you started to compete and you started to enjoy winning as well. I was never a great athlete, but I'm often told it is a nice feeling to win and get that feeling of being the best. It's important to understand that, although this is fine, it brings in another dimension to the game. Squash becomes more than just a way of enjoying yourself and having fun. It becomes important to win because it gives you recognition and respect from other people. Sometimes that becomes the focus – which can potentially be a problem. If you are focusing on being successful because of the recognition, you've made squash more complicated. All of a sudden there is a new agenda that interferes with your ability to 'just play'.

Socrates is famous for extolling the virtues of self-knowledge (Corlett, 1996). He says that knowing yourself is the most vital knowledge we can possibly attain. If you don't know yourself, how can you be yourself? If we are not ourselves, we are not going to achieve our potential (Csikszentmihalyi, 1990). Many athletes and players struggle to perform under pressure because they are conscious of what other people think or expect. In our society, many people live life in an emotional straightjacket because they are worried about what other people think, or what they might say. It could be argued that many England teams and British athletes crumble in major competitions because of pressure from the media. This is simply another illustration of how we can become paralysed by our concern over what other people think.

When the following elements come together, we stand a very good chance of finding *The Zone* or *Flow State*:

- If we know ourselves, and are genuinely happy with ourselves, we tend to be less concerned about what other people think of us.
- If we are sure of ourselves, other people's opinions have less impact.
- When we are sure of ourselves and our skills, we are free to trust ourselves to perform.
- When we trust, we think less and are able to *just play*.
- In this mindless (non-thinking) state, we are able to perform using our right-brain and we allow our bodies to move freely.
- We become immersed in the activity and operate in the moment.

These principles underpin peak performance. They are not modern. They have always been a part of human life and human performance. Recently researchers have started to document and study them (Young and Pain, 1999). As human beings we tend to research the things we see, create models and theories to explain them and then try to apply these back to practice. Therefore, coaching methods have been developed around some of these principles during the last 50 years or so (Gallwey, 1986). Some of these theories focus on coaching and learning (Robinson, 2006). Some focus on the psychology of peak performance (Jackson and Csikszentmihalyi, 1999). At their heart, most do not aim to add new techniques or skills. Instead, they aim to remove the inhibitions that stop people from performing naturally. We will explore these over the course of the coming chapters.

Once we can take control, we can genuinely start to produce optimal performances consistently. With this in mind, there are a host of conditions that need to be right for us to continually achieve a peak performance. Some of these require us to take a deep look at ourselves and make some significant shifts in thinking. I can't do that for you, but through the rest of this book I will do my best to lead you through the questions and challenges that make up the journey.

Summary

- *The Zone* is a state of complete focus, immersion and absorption in the task.
- We need to focus not only on what we do, but also on how we do it.
- There are some key ingredients: clear focus, a love for what you do, confidence, excitement and a good mood.
- We also need to strike a balance between the challenge and our skills.
- Most importantly, we need to be ourselves.

2

Your mind is like a Formula One car

A while ago I did some work with a very prestigious private bank in the UK. I worked with a group of senior partners on how to maximize their personal performance and the performance of the people around them. During one of the sessions I was asked: 'So, which is most important then, confidence, motivation or focus?'. To be honest I'd never been asked the question before so I had to stop and think for a minute. My brain tends to work in pictures and images. The image that entered my mind was a Formula One (F1) car. I started to realize that there are many key components in the car, all of which depend on each other. Having one on its own will not win you the race. Gradually, I started to explain how confidence, motivation and focus fit together, using the F1 car as an analogy.

Imagine the F1 car. It has an incredibly powerful and finely tuned engine. It's perfectly obvious to most of us that in order to produce the immense speeds required to win a race you need a powerful engine. However, a powerful engine alone will not win the race. A Dragster has a powerful engine, but it would not win the Monaco Grand Prix. Power is not the only quality that the car needs to possess. In order to win a race, our F1 car also requires manoeuvrability. Formula One races are not run on straight tracks. The cars need to have a state-of-the-art steering system in order to successfully navigate the course at high speed.

As we all know, even these two components are not enough to win. In fact, even if we went through every nut and bolt in the car we would still not find all the components required. In order to win a race, we need elements that lie outside the body of the car as well. Probably the most obvious is the driver. Arguably the driver is one of the most vital factors in the success of our F1 car. If we had the best engine on earth, the number one steering system and the finest nuts and bolts money could buy, we won't win the race with a timid driver who gets scared driving over 30 mph.

All this talk of F1 cars is all well and good, but how does it relate to our trio of confidence, motivation and focus? This is the way I see it:

- Motivation is the engine. It is sometimes known as 'drive'. It will provide us with the power and energy that we need.
- Focus is our steering system. Motivation alone is not enough. If our motivation is undirected, we won't achieve our goals. It is very easy to be a motivated, energetic fool who runs around doing all sorts of wonderful things that never produce an outcome. I have to say I've been guilty of that a few times myself.
- Confidence is our driver. Will the driver push himself and the car to the limits of its capacity, or back off a little at the crucial moments? Will the driver have enough confidence in the game plan to bide his time and only strike at exactly the right moment, or will he force a move that isn't there and spin off? Can the driver hold his nerve at crucial points in the race, or will he crack?

Maybe that's a long-winded way of saying you need all three. However, I think it's more than that. It shows that in reality they are dependent on each other – there is an interaction between the three components. In reality they all impact on each other. If they were colours, they would merge together as a spectrum rather than being individual blobs on a page.

If we look at the relationship between the three more closely, it's actually possible to see how they affect each other. When we have a simple, clear job, we have a very good chance of doing that job well (Donnelly and Ivancevich, 1975; Baumeister and Showers, 1986). Obviously, we need to have the knowledge, skills, resources and desire to do it as well. But, having a simple, clear task initially gives us a massive advantage. Evidence for this concept comes from a variety of sources. Researchers in management settings have identified that both task clarity (Lindsley et al., 1995) and role clarity (Bray and Brawley, 2002a, 2002b) have a significant impact on performance. When we understand the job, we're able to do it well. When we do the job well, we normally get a sense of satisfaction and fulfilment. Typically, as human beings, we like exhibiting mastery and we like to be successful in the things we do. So, when we perform well at something, we tend to want to do it again (Kloosterman, 1988). Psychologists such as Albert Bandura (1997) have identified strong links between mastery, confidence, achievement and motivation. These links set up our positive spiral:

- When I'm *focused* on a simple, clear job, I give myself the best chance of being successful.
- When I have done the job well I become *confident* and enjoy doing it.
- When I am confident in doing something, I am *motivated* to do it again.

These statements may seem perfectly obvious, but I do think that their significance is often over-looked. I've seen some very well-qualified managers who haven't recognized how important these fundamental principles are. They wonder why they have members of the team who seem unmotivated, but they don't look for the reasons why. If someone is not confident in their ability to do the job well, they might well shy away from it. Think about those tasks that you always seem to put off. Do they tend to be tasks that you'd consider easy and straightforward? Are they tasks that you're confident in, or are they the ones you're not sure about? Do they tend to be the tasks you are familiar with, or the ones you'd describe as more difficult or tricky?

The positive spiral that we've described also shows us how we can turn around under-performance or deteriorating performance (such as the one we looked at in the Introduction). It tells us that focus is often the best starting point. Most people would probably think that a lack of confidence might best be addressed head on. I have seen many football managers and coaches who believe that a pep talk is a good solution to a team's lack of confidence. I guess many people believe that giving someone a pep talk or increasing the amount of positive feedback they receive will help to boost their confidence. Equally, many people would probably think that an inspirational speech or a set of attractive incentives would boost motivation, but in reality they don't often have that effect. It does work in the movies – those famous speeches in films such as *Independence Day* and *Any Given Sunday* are iconic. However, in my experience, it doesn't often work the same way in practice and rarely has a significant and sustained effect on performance. In fact, research on performance spirals also indicates that verbal encouragement is not often enough to increase confidence or turn around a deteriorating performance (Lindsley et al., 1995).

I'd always start by trying to simplify the job. Cut out the complexity and start with a straightforward task that is entirely under the control of the performer (Horn, 2008). In a team environment, this means that everyone needs to have a simple job. They have to know what they need to do and how to do it. As a coach or manager, that is arguably our first job (Key, 2006). We will look at each of the three components in much more detail in the following chapters. For now, it's important to understand how they interact and relate to each other.

Here is an example from an equestrian rider I worked with recently:

It was lovely to meet you on Tuesday. We actually covered a lot of ground in just one hour. We started the session talking about your riding history. You said you've been riding since you were 6 and competing since about the age of 15. Interestingly, you described yourself as competing 'properly' since 2005 when you joined the team for the first time. It sounds like the journey has been a little up and down over the last few years because your original horse was injured in 2006. During the last few years, you have been really focused on getting back to where you were in 2005.

It's 2 weeks until the competition, which is obviously your big focus at the moment. It's probably fair to say that it is not just a big focus because it's in 2 weeks' time. In reality it represents your big ambition in the sport at this point and has been a focus for years. We discussed how you're feeling about it right now. Your words were 'scared, nervous and worried'. You also talked about the 'pressure of competing for this team in this competition'. We spent quite a while chatting about where this stems from. You talked about missing the opportunity in 2006 and not being ready in 2007. You also talked about the time and money invested into training and competition. You mentioned the pressure that you have perceived when competing for the team because there are people watching, etc. They are all common reasons why people feel nervous before events. In reality, what people do is they tend to attach a lot of meaning to an event, which acts as baggage and forms an agenda that is not really there.

As we continued to chat, we started to become aware of the even bigger issues that have been playing out. You mentioned that typically you have not been confident in yourself. This has manifested in your work and life. If we're not confident in life, we tend to pin all of our self-evaluation on the results we get from sport. In a sense, we look to our sporting success or failure to tell us how good we are at life. In this situation we rely on good results for our self-acceptance and therefore place massive pressure on the performance.

As I said, I believe that there is no such thing as pressure. It is created by our imagination. It has to be imaginary because it is a future event. The only place it can exist is our imagination. The fact is that because we create it, we can also get rid of it!

Ultimately, you will feel less pressure to perform in competition when you start to see it for what it really is – just you, the horse and some fences. The job is actually pretty simple when you look at it – jump over as many fences as you can as quickly as you can. If it starts to become more than that, we get into problems. The reality is that the job doesn't change just because it's a major competition. It wouldn't change if we put it into an arena with 100 TV cameras and called it an Olympic final or if it was a training session in your own paddock.

We talked about how you can build your confidence and become happy competing. As you said, priority number 1 is to have fun and enjoy it – that's the whole point in riding!! We also talked about how your performance is dependent upon your focus. If you are thinking 'I hope I don't hit the fence', then you're more likely to hit it. If you are thinking 'don't think about the blue pen', then your mind is fixed on the blue pen. The only way to turn this around is to start focusing on the things that will help you perform. As we chatted about it, you mentioned that focusing on the sound of the horses' hooves would be effective. If you can really immerse yourself in that sort of focus, your performance will start to take care of itself.

You also know that you can perform well. You have performed well recently (within the last couple of weeks) and cleared fences that you probably wouldn't have imagined you could clear. Your confidence is built upon evidence. Evidence tells you that you can clear the fences because you do it in training. If you can make training as challenging as competition, you will find it easier to see competition in the same way that you see training. Train like you compete and compete like you train!

In order to start turning their performance around, most people need a very simple starting point. They may see their task as bewildering, maybe even impossible. This is normally a result of getting the job wrong in the first place. We will explore this in much greater detail in Chapter 3. Simply understanding that our clarity of focus often underpins our confidence is the starting point and understanding that our confidence often underpins our motivation is the next stage.

Here is another example from a martial artist who was frustrated by his recent slump in form:

In order to help you to break the pattern that you are in, I asked you about the mental baggage that you're carrying at the moment. We started this by talking about why it is important to win. You said that winning was important because it tells you that you've done what you're capable of. This is important because you know that your training is coming together and you're heading in the right direction. I asked what the right direction is. You said 'becoming the British Champ'. I also asked why it's important to become the British Champ. You said that it proves to yourself and everyone else that you can do it. We started to talk about 'everyone else'. You started to tell me about your mates and the blokes at the gym. You also said that until you were 22 you were bullied and that being a martial arts champion would help you to counter that.

The problem is that it creates false pressure. It acts like a sack of bricks on your back, weighing you down. It clutters your mind and creates too much 'noise'. It stops you from doing the very, very simple job – fighting the best fight you can.

Fighting the best fight you can on the day is your *only* job. The job is not to win. It is not to qualify for anything. It is not to impress anyone or make anyone else happy or proud. Stick to a very simple, clear focus. We chatted briefly about the best point of focus for you. I asked you 'what is the single most important thing you need to focus on when you're fighting?'. You said – 'watch the opponent's eyes'.

Keep it simple, watch the opponent's eyes and let your instinct and skills do the rest.

These principles don't just apply to sports. They apply equally to any other walk of life. Here is an example from the first session of an Executive Coaching programme with the leader of a high profile business, who was frustrated because he was working a huge number of hours but struggling to move the business forward at the pace he desired:

You mentioned that although you know you should focus your attentions, you are easily distracted. It seems that the primary source of the distraction is the people around you. The dichotomy is that you want to be accessible and yet you need to focus. You know that it's important to be responsive to people so that they feel valued.

You obviously have a huge personal investment in the business and an emotional tie. The business really does matter to you. As a result, it sounds like you wear your heart on your sleeve to a certain extent. You have deliberately sought to create a culture that is built on honesty, authenticity and transparency. The flip side of the coin is that people see when you're up and down, and it also has an impact on them.

I asked the question 'if you had a magic wand, how would things look?'. You started by saying that there really aren't enough hours in the day. You need to start focusing on your workload and being effective with your time. As we discussed this, you mentioned in passing that you are a 'bit of a control freak'. In the same breath, you also said that all of your directors are better than you in their respective fields. You trust them and are happy to let them run with projects. However, you also get yourself sucked into meetings that you may not need to be in.

In our ideal picture we see you with more strategic thinking time and strategic execution time. You are less involved in proofreading, answering questions that aren't yours and in the minutiae and meetings that don't involve you. We also discussed a future where you work closely with your directors to drive corporate objectives. You mentioned spending more time on your visible external profile, winning new clients and exploring market opportunities. It would also allow you to take a more strategic look at the internal structure and culture within the business.

All of this can be summed up with the phrase 'not doing the doing'. In the 'plan–do–review' cycle, your role is to focus on the plan and review elements. We talked about the transition to a 'hands-free' business and the need to ensure that the business could run itself if you were run over by a bus. As a friend of mine once said, you judge a personal fitness trainer on how their client performs when they are not there.

Step 1 is to clarify and simplify your role to ensure that you can be as effective as possible. We need to sharpen your focus so that you know exactly where you should direct your energies to have the maximum possible impact. Once we do that, you stand a very good chance of both reducing the number of hours at your desk *and* making more of an impact on the business.

Our next step is also to look in detail at how we sharpen focus, control our point of focus and ensure that we're focusing on the most effective things.

Summary

- Focus, confidence and motivation are all fundamental to peak performance.
- They are interdependent. They require each other.
- Focus underpins confidence.
- Confidence underpins motivation.
- To turn around a performance, it is often wise to start by clarifying our focus.

3

Razor sharp focus

> Progress has little to do with speed, but much to do
> with direction.
>
> (Anon)

What is it that makes the difference between the true
greats and the 'also-rans'? Is it talent? Is it determination
and drive? Is it attitude? In reality it is probably a combination of all of these and more. Over the years I have
worked with a lot of athletes, from those at the very
pinnacle of their sport, to junior athletes learning the
ropes. No matter what level, there is something that
successful athletes have in common – their ability to focus!

True champions show an incredible level of long-term
focus (Jones and Moorhouse, 2007). They work consistently
for years and years to perfect their performance. Many
world class athletes were pretty average in their early
years. At age 10, they might be relatively talented but they
don't tend to stick out from the pack. However, those who
go on to become champions will probably already be starting to set themselves apart at an early age. Day on day the
true champions will practise a little longer, work a little
harder and push themselves further (Colvin, 2008). They
will be incredibly focused on their sport and dedicate
themselves to refining the tiny details day after day for
years and years. If they became 0.1 per cent better than
their opposition each day, it wouldn't take long before

there was a noticeable gap. This long-term focus starts to create champions (England & Wales Cricket Board, 2005).

It is long-term focus that Olympians require to drive them through multiple 4-year preparation cycles (Johnson, 1996). They can go months without a major competition, so they need incredible focus to keep training to the highest level. However, it's not just Olympians who need long-term focus. It is easy for a professional athlete to get lost in a busy season. Professional players in all sports often move from one match to the next without really stopping to focus on what they are supposed to be working on. Just playing the matches won't make you a champion. Professional players have to constantly improve their game, refine their skills and learn from each performance.

Obviously this is not just true in sports. It applies equally to all areas of life. It is not possible to develop excellence in anything overnight. It isn't possible to build a successful business or organization overnight either. True success takes a great deal of time, effort and investment, consistently delivered over a long period. In many cases, there is a guiding vision behind it all. It could be the vision of an organization's founder. It is often driven by someone's dream. Examples can be seen in biographies of business founders, such as Fred Smith, the founder of FedEx (Trimble, 1993).

If you listen to interviews with athletes just after they win medals, many will say that 'it is a dream come true'. They've probably been imagining that moment since childhood. Their dream has been fuelling their motivation, which gets them out of bed at a ridiculous time of the morning for years on end (Torres and Weil, 2009). It keeps them going when they're in pain and pushes them through their dark times. Perhaps, more importantly, it also helps them focus on what they need to do every day in order to achieve that dream: 'I dream my painting and then I paint my dream' (Vincent Van Gogh).

Having a dream or a vision is great. However, we need to know how to turn that dream into a tangible reality. We have to know exactly what we need to do today and tomorrow in order to get us close to achieving the dream. If we simply keep dreaming, we will just be a dreamer. We need to *do*, in order to achieve.

Many people have a real challenge converting their dream or their vision into reality. The challenge lies in the fact that the dream or vision is often an outcome. It is often a result. For example, a football manager dreams of winning the Champions League, an athlete dreams of Olympic gold, an entrepreneur dreams of having a multi-billion-dollar business empire. They are all outcomes. Although the outcome may be our driver and our motivator, focusing on it may actually be counter-productive. If we focus on the outcome, we often fail to focus on the things we need to do to achieve it. By focusing on the outcome, we often forget to focus on the processes that will get us there. This principle underpins business improvement models such as Six Sigma (Keller, 2009) and Kaizen (Imai, 1986).

I worked with a swimmer for around 8 years. When we started working together, he was a decent National standard athlete who had just competed at the World Student Games but had not yet won a full Great Britain (GB) cap. He dreamt of winning Olympic gold in his favoured event: the 100 metres breaststroke. For the first 3 years or so we worked in a slight fog. We were making progress to a certain extent but, to be honest, the plan we were working to was a 'best guess'. We were a little bit reactionary. It almost felt like we were navigating in very poor visibility and were reacting as things appeared. At the time, we were working to a set of goals that included 'making the GB team', 'securing funding', 'securing sponsorship', 'qualifying for championships', 'winning key races', etc. After about 3 years we came to a stark realization. To that point we had made a fundamental error. We had got the job wrong. His job was not to make the GB team. It wasn't to secure funding or sponsorship. It wasn't to qualify for championships or win races. He was a 100 metre swimmer in a 50 metre pool. His job was very, very simple. The job was to swim two lengths of the pool as quickly as he could.

That realization was like a blinding flash of light. It made an enormous impact on how we worked, our effectiveness and our end results. Immediately we started to identify exactly what he needed to do in order to swim two lengths of the pool as quickly as he could. He pulled together a team of specialists, including his coach, physiotherapist, bio-mechanist, performance analyst, nutritionist, physiologist, strength and conditioning coach and performance-lifestyle advisor. Everyone was challenged to help him swim two lengths of the pool as quickly as he possibly could. We broke down his stroke. We analyzed his technique. He started to figure out what the key elements of his performance were and put programmes in place to improve them. He changed his training regime to take out many of the things he habitually did (because they had always been on the programme) and replaced them with things that would contribute to swimming two lengths quicker. In came yoga, gymnastics and specialist physiotherapy work to improve his streamlining. Out went some of the swim sessions and strength sessions that may not have been contributing. We spent 2–3 years working on a project to help improve his starts by a few tenths of a second and another to work on his turns. We analyzed his performances to find the perfect race strategy for him and then put a programme in place to practise this and perfect it.

His whole outlook changed once we figured out what his real job was. It became a benchmark and a filter. Before doing anything, he would ask 'will this help me swim two lengths of the pool quicker?'. If it would make him quicker, he'd consider doing it. If not, it would be binned. We also started asking whether it was likely to knock a whole second off his time or 0.000001 seconds off. Obviously, the things that made the biggest impact had a higher priority.

This thought process set up our working practice for the last 4 or 5 years of his career. It helped him to become infinitely more focused, more effective and more successful. Because he could swim two lengths of the pool more quickly, he won more races, became a regular on the British team (and in fact became British number one for several years), qualified for major championships, made finals at World Championships and the Olympic Games and won two gold medals at the Commonwealth Games. He finished his career as the seventh fastest person in history in his event.

This all probably seems blatantly obvious to you. Why hadn't we thought of this sooner? Well, I'm certainly not claiming to be particularly clever. We probably should have realized it a lot earlier. However, most people rarely stop and think about what their job really is. Many of us know our dream. We have the vision. However, most people do what Chris and I did for the first 3 years. We just followed the daily pattern. Like most athletes, he did what it said on the schedule. I guess it becomes habit and to a certain extent you accept it and just fall into the pattern. We may not stop and actually check that everything we are doing is actually taking us towards our dream via the most effective possible route. Therefore, there is a gap between what we are doing right now and our dream.

In recent years, I have started to apply these principles to my performance coaching work outside of sport. I know the enormous positive impact it had when we discovered Chris' 'two lengths of the pool'. Therefore, I now encourage everyone to understand their own '2 Lengths': What is your 2 Lengths of the pool? What is your job in the simplest possible terms? Here are a few examples that have come from applying this exercise to both groups and individuals:

100 metre breaststroke swimmer in a 50 metre pool
'Swim 2 Lengths of the baths as quickly as I can.'
Javelin thrower
'Throw the javelin as far as I can down the field.'
Olympic archer
'Get as many of my arrows as close to the centre of the target as I can.'
A soccer team
'Score as many goals as possible and concede as few as possible.'
Law firm
'Deliver outstanding legal business solutions with high profitability.'
Bakery
'Sell as many exceptional quality bakery products as possible profitably.'
An insurance sales team
'Generate high-quality leads and convert them to repeating sales.'
PR/communications company
'Use communications to achieve the business aims of the client profitably.'
Managing partner of a law firm
'Create the strategy and structure to deliver £X million in fees profitably.'
Business development director of the same law firm
'Maximize the income of the business through selling legal services.'
Managing director of PR/communications company
'Focus the business to deliver its 2 Lengths.'

You may have noticed that there is a theme to many of these. There is a set of guidelines that they all conform to:

1   It needs to be a process, not an outcome.
2   It has to be entirely within your control.

3   It should fit neatly after the words 'My/our job is to . . .'.
4   It needs to be very specific.
5   We need to know that if we achieve the 2 Lengths, we've accomplished the job completely.

Let's take a look at Chris's definition again in more detail. His job is to:

- *Swim*
  Not run, walk, cycle, canoe or any other method of propulsion.
- *2 Lengths of the pool*
  He's not particularly bothered if he's not the fastest after 50 m and he doesn't need to be able to do miles in the pool.
- *as quickly*
  He is measured by time, not profit or distance or any other marker.
- *as he can*
  He is not trying to swim quicker than everyone else, because that's not within his control. He has not set a target (i.e. in under 60 seconds), because that's also pretty arbitrary. If he swam under 60 seconds but it wasn't the fastest he could swim, he will not have produced his best. If he swims the fastest he possibly can and it's 60.1 seconds, he couldn't swim any quicker. His only job is to swim as fast as he can on the day, and to try and be quicker today than he was yesterday, and quicker tomorrow than he is today.

Let's have a look at the law firm in the same way. Their 2 Lengths is to:

- *Deliver*
  They are a practice, so they need to be delivering services to clients.

- *outstanding*
  Not average or 'pretty good' or even 'good'.
- *legal business solutions*
  They are a law firm specializing in the business/ commercial sector (not family law or criminal law or probate law). They focus on providing a solution for the client (i.e. a service that aids the client and solves a problem for them).
- *with high profitability*
  Because if they don't, they will not be performing as a business.

Once you've found your 2 Lengths, stress test it to make sure it's robust and it stands up to challenge. Make sure that it really is your job and that by delivering your 2 Lengths you will ultimately be successful. For example, if your 2 Lengths is related to business performance, it should probably make some reference to profit. If whatever you are doing is not profitable, you won't be in business long. Equally, for charities, operating within budget should arguably be in the 2 Lengths somewhere. If not, you're not going to be operating very long either.

Fred Smith, founder of FedEx, often refers to the *one thing* that the business is there to do. He advocates knowing the *one thing* and sticking to it (Trimble, 1993).

So, once you've found your 2 Lengths, what is the next step? The next step is to look at *how* you deliver it. In my work, I ask clients to identify the five most important and significant factors that will help them deliver their 2 Lengths. If they could only have a list of five, what would those five be? Because I'm a sport psychologist and performance coach, I decided to give these five things a snazzy title: *5 Keys to Success*.

There is a good reason why I ask for a maximum of five. We can just about focus on five things, but we'd struggle to really deliver against more than five. We'd get a law of diminishing returns and we wouldn't really do them justice if we tried to address more than five. If we have less than five, that's okay. A list of three is fine by me. The problem comes when we have too many things. Our brain simply can't do it (Richtel, 2010). Often, just simplifying the job helps us to be successful (Trout and Rivkin, 1998).

I worked with one of the Great Britain Olympic squads just after they returned from the Beijing Games in 2008. They had had a disappointing Games and had returned empty handed. It was slightly unexpected because their previous Olympic performance was pretty good. The athletes were very capable and they had one of the world's most respected coaches. In one of our first meetings, I asked the coach to list the five most significant factors that would impact on the athletes' performance: 'What are the five things that they really need to do? If they could only do five things, which would be the most crucial five?' As I asked the coach the questions, he looked at me perplexed. He then proceeded to draw up a list of 32 crucial factors that each athlete absolutely had to do in order to perform well. All of a sudden it became clear to me why these athletes had not performed. The greatest mind on the planet could not focus on getting 32 things right all at once. As I challenged him to reduce the list he became adamant that you could not prioritize just five. In talking to the athletes, it became obvious that they were very unclear about what they needed to do to perform well. When they stood on the line, their mind was whirring with the long list of things they needed to do. As a result, they under-performed and became confused, frustrated and disillusioned. A skill that had once been second nature to them had become complex and difficult.

Have a look at your 2 Lengths. What are your *5 Keys to Success*? What are the five things that, if you do them, will almost guarantee you success? They have to be the five most significant factors – the five that will have the greatest impact on your performance and will deliver your 2 Lengths. It's worth spending time to ensure that you are happy with your 5 Keys. When we get the process right, we should be able to apply almost all of our focus to our 5 Keys. If we deliver these 5 Keys to the best of our ability, we will almost certainly deliver our 2 Lengths. If we have our 2 Lengths right, we know that we will be successful when we deliver them.

So that we have absolute confidence in our 5 Keys, I recommend stress testing them to make sure that they stand up to scrutiny. Here is a little guide that I put together for the senior management team of a corporation recently. The guide was designed to help them stress test their organization's 5 Keys and their departmental 5 Keys:

1   Are you happy with the organization's 5 Keys? If you deliver these, will you deliver the organization's 2 Lengths?

2   Are you confident that by delivering your department's 5 Keys you will contribute to the organization's 5 Keys (and therefore the 2 Lengths)? Or, do you need to deliver your 5 Keys plus the organization's 5 Keys (i.e. focus on 10 in total)? If it's the latter, we need to re-think your 5 Keys and align them to the organization more closely.

3   How will you assess/evaluate the delivery of your department's 5 Keys? Can you score yourself on a scale of 1–10 on your current performance of the 5 Keys (i.e. today we're a 6/10)?

4   Can you describe how a score that is 2 higher than your current score differs from your performance right now (i.e. the difference between an 8/10 and your current 6/10)? How different will an 8/10 look, sound, feel, think and act? If you struggle to do this, your 5 Keys might be too general or too vague to be deliverable.

5   Do your 5 Keys reflect the most significant elements (i.e. those that will have the biggest impact on your performance) in delivering the 2 Lengths?

   a   Have you tested the sixth and seventh most significant against the top five?
   b   Is there anything that would stop you committing to delivering these five?
   c   Is there anything more important/higher priority?

If there are higher priorities than your 5 Keys, it means that whatever you'd see as a higher priority should be one of your five! Remember, the 5 Keys should be those things that have the biggest impact on your performance.

Of course, this process applies equally to a sports team with its various units (i.e. attack, defence, midfield, etc) and positions (Key, 2006). Once you know these five, you have a very effective set of things to focus on. The next stage of the challenge is to control your focus on the things that will give you your best performance. So, how do you control focus?

When I work with athletes, I often describe focus as a torch beam (Taylor and Wilson, 2005; Taylor, 2010). In reality, our focus is similar to a narrow beam. We are really only able to focus on one thing at a time. Often we will think that we are focusing on 100 different things, because our mind seems to be full to bursting point. However, we actually only focus on one at a time and dart between the various things that are in our minds, spending very little time actually dedicated to any one. Our torch beam hops between those thoughts that are competing for our attention, and only settles on any one of them for a moment before dashing off to the next (Weissman, Roberts, Visscher and Woldorff, 2006; Hamilton, 2008).

The challenge for many athletes is actually to take control of the torch and decide where the beam will shine. What is it that you need to focus on? Once you know, you need to take a hold of the torch and make sure you direct your beam and keep it steady. It's tough to do at times. A lot of us don't have the mental discipline required to hold our focus for any prolonged period. We are easily distracted and find that something draws the torch beam. This tends to be exacerbated if we're scared (Horn, 2008). Imagine walking along a path in the dark with a narrow torch beam. If you are scared, you react differently. If you hear something go bump behind you, the likelihood is that you'll spin round and shine your torch on it to see what made the noise. This draws your beam from the path you are supposed to be following. If you were comfortable walking the path, or you could see pretty clearly, you would be much less likely to take your beam off the path.

In sport, if we're not feeling confident we tend to start over-thinking (Rotella, 2005). This draws our focus (Blanke, 2007). A tennis player should arguably be 100 per cent focused on the ball. If she's not focused on the ball, the chances of playing a decent shot are pretty remote. If the player is thinking about the mistake she made in her last shot (instead of shining her torch on the ball), her torch will be shining on her own thoughts. When we over-think, we experience what I call 'thought blindness'. Imagine a batsman in cricket facing a fast bowler who delivers a ball at 90 mph. The batsman has to select a shot and execute it in a split second (Cork, Justham and West 2008). Thinking takes a relatively long time. If the batsman thinks, he will not see the bowler or the ball clearly because his brain will be tied up with his thoughts and will not be registering those things his eyes are seeing. The only way for the batsman to play a good shot is to simply watch the bowler and the ball as closely as possible and let his unconscious mind play the shot. The batsman has to be in a 'mindless' state (Rotella, 2005).

Many players do need to think at times. They may need to decide where to play shots and how to play their game tactically. However, when it comes to executing the shot, thinking will tend to interfere (Gallwey, 1986). Our 'non-thinking', unconscious mind controls our movement. If we want to play great shots, we have to feel the shots, see the shots and hear the shots. We can't think them. To be in 'the zone' we need to be totally absorbed in what we're doing, to the exclusion of everything else. The more intensely we can immerse ourselves in the shot, the greater our chances of entering 'the zone'. When we engage our senses fully, we will start to immerse ourselves and become absorbed in the shots. In order to do this, we need to be able to control our focus (Cziksentmihalyi, 1990).

For years I have heard people ask: 'How do I stop thinking negative thoughts?' The answer is alarmingly simple. Focus on something else. If you try not to think about something, the chances are you will think about it even more. Here's a challenge. Don't think about the word *blue*. Don't think about *the colour blue*. Don't think about *blue* things. Think about anything except BLUE. What are you thinking?

The only way to stop thinking about blue is to start focusing on RED. Red roses? Red Ferraris? Red anything. The same is true of negative thoughts. The way to stop thinking them is to start focusing on something else. You do this naturally when you're confident. That's why you play better when you're confident. Confidence and focus are closely linked. If you can control confidence, focus will automatically become easier. Control your focus. Choose to focus on something that will help you play better (Anderson, 2000). Arguably the best way to focus on our performance is to engage our senses (McKim, 1980; Gallwey, 1986; Cook, 2005; Rauch, 2010), particularly your three primary senses in sport. Focus on what you see, hear and feel. Here are some very personal examples from athletes:

Martial artist
• Watch the opponent's eyes.

International squash player
• Watch the movement on the ball.
• Feel the shots.
• Hear the sound that your shots are making or the sound of your footwork.

Hammer thrower
• Feel the balance in your feet.
• Hear the sound of your rhythm.
• Feel the smoothness in your movement.

Tennis player
• Watch the ball and pick it up as early as possible (as your opponent plays the shot, rather than as the ball comes over the net).
• Feel 'lightness' in your feet and hear the sound of your footwork.

Golfer
• Hear the sound of the club hitting the ball.
• Feel your balanced start position.
• Close your eyes to stop yourself following the ball.

Javelin thrower
• Feel the solidity of the front leg (and knee).
• Hear the sound of the rhythm in the approach run.

These are the points of focus that the athletes felt would give them the best performance. It's important to focus rather than think. We need to notice, rather than analyze.

It's easy to start analyzing how something feels. If we do this, we could start messing up our technique because our thinking brain starts to try to control our movement. Noticing allows us to simply observe and be aware of these sensory cues, without feeling the need to control or change them. Our subconscious mind will execute the skills. We simply need to see, hear, feel and trust (Gallwey, 1986)!

The same principles apply outside of sport. Although we may not have the same need to see, hear and feel a performance, we will need to focus on the 5 Keys that will ensure we deliver our own 2 Lengths of the pool. We need to keep our focus on the processes and make sure we deliver them. When we consistently deliver the processes, the outcomes will inevitably follow. If not, we probably need to review the 5 Keys that we selected. But how do we keep the torch on those key things?

Firstly, we need to recognize that focus follows interest (Gallwey, 2003). If we're more interested in winning than performing well, this can affect our focus. If we're losing, our torch beam will start to settle on our doubts and negative thoughts. Our mind will be dominated by thoughts such as 'what if I don't win' or 'I can't see how I'm going to win this'. If we're genuinely more interested in performing well, it is easier to focus on the things that will help us perform well (i.e. what we need to see, hear or feel).

Our interest will also be heightened if we strike the balance between the perceived challenge and our perception of our skills (Cziksentmihalyi, 1990). Peak performances (also known as 'flow') occur when our view of the challenge and our belief in our skills are both high. This state requires us to focus. If we don't have the stimulus from the challenge, it is unlikely to grab our attention. We know this from our own experience. When we are engaged in something challenging, we need to give it our full attention and we tend to become immersed in the task. This will only remain as long as we can engage with the

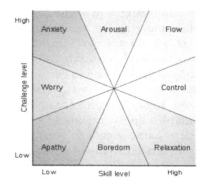

Figure 3.1 The challenge and skills balance (Csikszentmihalyi,
2008), reproduced from *Flow: The Psychology of
Optimal Experience* by Mihaly Csikszentmihalyi.
Copyright © 1990 Mihaly Csikszentmihalyi.
Reprinted by permission of Mihaly Csikszentmihalyi
and HarperCollins Publishers.

task successfully. If our skills are not up to the challenge,
then we'll quickly get frustrated and lose interest. If the
challenge is far beyond our perceived skills, we might end
up becoming anxious. This balance between our skills and
the challenge is depicted in Figure 3.1.

You can practise controlling your focus and holding your
focus on specific cues. Sports players can do this in training. They can select one of their key points of focus and
lock onto it. There will be a whole host of things that will
try to draw your focus. Some of these will be external (such
as the opposition or referee) and some will be internal
(such as your own thoughts or doubts). The challenge is to
bring your focus back to those highly effective cues as soon
as you can. What should you be focusing on? What should
you be seeing, hearing or feeling (Cook, 2005)?

Outside of sport, the same principles apply. Often I
challenge people to keep tabs on how much of their time
has been spent delivering their 5 Keys and their own 2

Lengths. Sometimes we use simple exercises to outline the activities they do in the course of their working days. We then categorize these as 'core activities', 'support activities' or 'distractions'. I define core activities as those that directly contribute to your 2 Lengths. The support activities help you to do the core activities better, although they may not in themselves be classed as 'core'. Finally, 'distractions' do not contribute to the 2 Lengths and actually may detract from it. In addition to knowing which activities fall into each category, we can also estimate how much time, energy and focus goes into each. This gives us a simple means of assessing effectiveness.

Focus is the cornerstone of our performance. We need to have a simple, clear focus first. If we have a simple, clear focus, we're likely to be able to perform. Once we perform well, we will become more confident. When we're confident, we are likely to be motivated to do it again. Performance starts with simplicity and clarity.

Summary

- Focus is the foundation. Simplify and clarify!
- Focus on the processes.
- Find your '2 Lengths' and '5 Keys'.
- Focus is like a torch beam.
- Identify the most effective processes to focus on, and hone in.
- If you want to stop thinking about X, start focusing on Y.
- Focus through your senses; see, hear and feel the performance.

4

Control your confidence

I worked for a few years in Premiership football. I often heard the manager and coaches saying 'if we could just win a couple of games, we'd get our confidence back and then we'll start playing well'. I've been fortunate to have worked in a huge variety of sports during the past 15 years and one thing I've noticed is that confidence is the Holy Grail for most athletes. Most athletes recognize that when they are confident they perform well. They think less and play a more natural, and normally effortless, game. It's equally true outside of sport. I've spoken to numerous sales directors and senior sales managers who have told me 'sales is 90 per cent confidence'. However, as those football managers highlighted, finding your confidence is often thought of as a 'chicken and egg thing'. Without the confidence you're unlikely to perform well, but you need a good performance to feel confident . . . or do you? As a performance coach, I teach people to take control of their confidence.

I recently worked with a sales team who were not performing consistently. When I discussed the issue with the sales executives, many of them described a very simple pattern. When they were selling they were confident and they sold more. When they weren't selling their confidence took a hit and they struggled. I liken this to centre forwards in a football team. When they are scoring they are confident and they score more. When their confidence is low they become 'shot shy' and therefore they don't take as many shots and consequently don't score as many goals.

This is a fragile system and one where the performer (the salesperson or the centre forward in these examples) is not in control. They are essentially relying on circumstance to provide them with 'a bit of luck'. When our performance is reliant on external factors (other people or circumstances), we are in a position of weakness.

Where does confidence come from? Confidence comes from evidence (Bandura, 1997). The reason that you're confident tying your shoelaces is because you have done it hundreds of times before and been consistently successful. You have the evidence. Most of us would be less confident if we were asked to climb Mount Everest. The simple fact is that our bank of evidence doesn't tell us we've done it and been successful on numerous occasions. In fact, for the majority of the population, we can't say we've climbed similar peaks or had experience of climbing in the Himalayas. As a result, we probably wouldn't be particularly confident we could achieve it. If we take this logic a step further, evidence tells us that even experienced climbers find Everest challenging (Clash, 2003). How confident do you think we would feel if we believe we have consistently failed in a particular task? We have a real challenge if our bank of evidence tells us that we will probably fail again. So what's the solution?

I hear many people trying to affect someone's confidence with a 'pep talk' or by giving positive feedback. In business and sport, managers and coaches will often try to persuade someone that they have the ability. A coach might point towards recent good performances or results. A manager might remind a team member of successes they'd had in the past. I have found that this is quite common in sales environments. The aim, of course, is to help the person to see the positive evidence, which will then hopefully increase their confidence. Occasionally it might have an effect. Often the effect will be fairly short lived and fragile. However, it does highlight an important point. Our confidence comes from the evidence that we *see*. The fact that evidence exists is not enough. We have to see it and recognize it if it is to have an impact and actually build our confidence. Some people appear to be 'naturally confident', whereas others don't. In reality, those who appear naturally confident probably look for and see evidence of their ability. It doesn't mean that they have more ability, but they look for the evidence and therefore see the evidence more readily than others (Branden, 1984, 2001).

I once worked with a gymnast. She was 16 years old and one of the highest ranked gymnasts in the country. Most people would agree that she was very good. However, she had incredibly low self-confidence. She did not think she was good. In one of our first sessions I watched her complete an exercise in training. She called the exercise a 'circuit' and she performed it on the beam. The circuit involved five different skills, performed five times each (i.e. 25 discrete skills in total). As I watched, I noticed that she would occasionally stop and make notes in a note book. At the end of the circuit I asked her what she was writing. 'I write down all my mistakes', she said. When we evaluated her performance together, there was one imperfection in each of the different skills, but she only produced that imperfection once in the five attempts. Therefore, of the 25 attempts, only five had an imperfection. In reality, 80 per cent was perfect. When we discussed the degree of the imperfections, it turned out that the 'imperfect' attempts were probably rated at about 8/10 (i.e. 80 per cent correct). The mistakes (as she called them) were certainly not catastrophic. In reality they were simply not 100 per cent perfect. Of all of the evidence available, the gymnast was choosing to look at the imperfections. She was looking purely at her mistakes. She only saw what she could not do. As a result, her perception was dominated by mistakes and so she concluded that she wasn't any good.

'We see in the world what we look for' (Anon) – knowing this, it is important that we look for solid sources of evidence on which to build our confidence (Dayton, 2007). What do you think most people's confidence is under-pinned by? The answer for most people is 'results'. How-ever, that's not a strong position to be in. If your confidence is reliant upon winning or losing, it is going to be fragile. Winning or losing is something you cannot directly control. There are a huge number of factors that dictate the result. Although you have a certain degree of control, you can't control everything that influences a result. In sport, for example, the referee normally has an enormous influence on results. Do you really want refereeing decisions to influence your confidence? In sales, the customer arguably has the biggest influence. Although a sales executive can do a fantastic job of positioning a product or service, they cannot make the decision for the customer. In the sales scenario there are hundreds of factors outside of the sales executive's control that will ultimately influence the decision.

Aside from results, most people's confidence is influ-enced by a host of other external factors. The more common ones are 'coach or manager feedback', 'other people's feedback' or, for juniors particularly, 'parent feedback'.

I worked with a footballer a few years ago who was lacking confidence. We chatted about what influenced his confidence. The manager had the biggest influence, followed by other players, the crowd, his Dad and even the newspaper report. When we looked at it objectively, it was likely that the manager's feedback was not going to be completely reliable. The manager will be watching 20+ players on the field and not really focusing on him. If his team wins, the manager is likely to be happy with him. If they lose, he won't. That also goes for the other players, the crowd and the newspaper. As we chatted, it became apparent that the player's own views counted for very little. Ironically, of course, the player himself was in the best position to review his game and probably had the most accurate feedback. He'd seen and felt his performance from inside his body. However, he'd given control of his confidence over to everyone else. As a result, his confidence wasn't based on his own performance; it was based on how everyone else felt. That's not a great position to be in.

This example shows that controlling confidence often starts with how we control feedback. Our footballer started to control his confidence when he started to honestly and objectively evaluate his own performance. It sounds very simple and straightforward, but let's take a look in more detail.

Firstly, he needs to be honest. If he has had a poor game, he needs to be honest about it. Equally, if he has played really well, he needs to be honest rather than modest. Most people struggle with this stage. We are either too harsh on ourselves or look for excuses. This feedback is only for our own benefit. What is the point in being anything other than completely honest? The only one who will suffer the consequences of dishonesty is ourself.

Secondly, our player needs to be objective. The player needs to use his own evaluation and then integrate feedback from others. The aim is not to be arrogant and ignore the feedback of others. However, we shouldn't rely completely on the feedback from others. We should have our own view. We need to be able to provide ourselves with objective feedback on a performance. I have worked with a lot of athletes and business people who rely completely on their coach or manager for feedback. Like any state of dependency, this puts us in a potential position of weakness. The strongest position is to use the benefit of both viewpoints and integrate the feedback of others with our own objective views. These views should not be driven by emotion, but by the evidence. We should look at our performance as a whole, not just focus on the two or three things that went either particularly well or badly. Many athletes fall into the trap of thinking the whole performance was horrendous because of one error that cost them the match. In reality, that is not an objective evaluation; it is an emotional reaction. If our feedback is based on a negative emotional reaction, our confidence will probably suffer. We should not ignore the error or pretend that it was okay, but we do need to put it in context with the rest of the performance so that we get a fair and proper view.

Finally, our player needs to evaluate the performance. Most players don't evaluate, they judge. Normally the judgement is emotionally charged and contains little in the way of useful information. How many times have you described a performance as 'good', 'ok' or '****'. None of these judgements have any value. They will not help you become better. They will not improve your performance or help you to engineer your confidence. When I work with athletes, I often start by asking them to rate their performance on a scale of 0–10. It's never going to be a zero. There will always be something in it that was positive. Equally, it's very rare that a performance would be a 'perfect' (flawless) 10. Whatever you score, there will always be two elements to your score. What did you do well (which stopped you from scoring zero)? What can you improve (which stopped you from scoring 10)? Knowing these two things will help you ensure that your next performance is better than this one.

'But what happens if I scored a 2? Surely I'm not going to be confident going into the next game' I hear you ask. That depends on how you decide to respond to a 2/10 score. One response would be to feel disheartened and start to convince yourself that you're rubbish. The other response is to work on all the things that need improving. Start on the training ground. Start by getting the basics nailed down, and then build and build until you start to become more confident that you can deliver. There is a very simple formula that you can use to create confidence – build on what you can do!

In the spring I sat down with a junior international archer. I asked why she looked troubled. She told me she was dreading school, particularly Business Studies. I challenged her to tell me five questions that she would love to see on the exam paper because she knew the answers inside out. Initially she told me she didn't have any. After a little grouching and muttering she agreed to think about it overnight. Next day she said she had seven questions. 'Great', I said, 'Your job now is to research five more questions so that you know them inside out too. You need to know them so well that you'd love to see them on the exam paper. Once you know these five new questions, you'll have 12.' I then asked her how confident she would feel if she had 150 questions that she'd love to see on the exam paper. Of course, she'd feel confident. So, the formula is simple. Once you've got 12, research another five, then another five until you have enough to feel truly confident. She got a B in her exam – well done!

Here is an excerpt from a report that I wrote for a female junior tennis player following a review session. In the session, she told me that she'd rated one of her performances as a 5/10. Her initial reaction was to become frustrated and lose confidence. However, there is an opportunity to use the performance to increase her confidence by working on the weaknesses until she becomes confident in those areas of her game.

> You said that your opponent served faster and with more spin. She was a left-handed player and served wide. The spin made the ball bounce up in front of you, which caused you a challenge. In addition, she returned deep off your serve, which also made things more difficult for you.

We talked about how you can change your game to cope with this challenge. I'm a great believer in attacking challenges like this and making sure you can become comfortable with them. The only way to do that is to train these elements of your game. It sounds as if your training partner Jonny can really help to challenge you. He has a strong left-handed serve and can put spin on the shot. He is 2 years older than you and he's a bloke. If you can cope comfortably with Jonny's serve, I'll bet you can cope with tough-serving girls you'd meet in competition. If you knew you could cope with Jonny's serve comfortably, how confident would you feel facing a similar opponent in competition next time? If you use this experience and work on your game, you can actually increase your confidence in the long run.

You can use the same simple principles to control your own confidence. Start with what you're doing well and add to it. Practise the bits you're not as confident in until you know you can do them. I often speak to athletes just before they embark on major competitions. As you can imagine, confidence is often a natural topic of conversation. There are a variety of sources from which elite performers draw their confidence (Hayes, Maynard, Thomas and Bawden, 2007). However, it probably won't come as any great surprise to you that there is a recurring theme with these conversations. When performers feel more prepared, they are likely to be more confident (Orlick, 2000; Horn, 2008). Good preparation gives us the evidence that we can perform well. This is true not only in sports. McDonald, Orlick and Letts (1995) found exactly the same with surgeons. Imagine two scenarios. The first is a scenario in which a swimmer has had an almost perfect training cycle leading up to a major competition. They have been hitting very good times in training and their 'warm-up' competitions. They feel strong, fast, lean and powerful. During the cycle they have made some significant technical changes and have started to see a positive impact on their performances. How confident do you think they will feel?

Let's compare that to a swimmer who has been plagued by injury and illness throughout the cycle. They have struggled to get a coherent period of uninterrupted training and don't feel like they have fully tested their body yet. As a result, they haven't been able to enter many of the warm-up competitions and say that they're feeling a little 'race rusty'. How confident are they likely to feel?

I know that these two examples are at opposite ends of the scale but this principle applies across the board. Image that one of our athletes has really focused on their training during the last 3 or 4 months. They have started to work on the fine details of their technique and have pushed themselves further than ever before in their sessions. In their heart of hearts they know that the last cycle has been their best yet and they have made substantial progress as a result. Let's compare this athlete to an athlete who has approached the last 3 or 4 months in the same way they have always done – they turn up and follow the session they are given. Normally if the coach asks for 100 per cent they give about 90, always leaving a little in reserve. They also have a tendency to drift off in a session and don't really focus on the details. Although they complete the sessions, they don't get the maximum possible benefit. Some of what they do will be good, but a lot will be sloppy. What impact do you think this will have on the athlete's confidence?

I often hear how confident an athlete is when I speak to them. Some athletes will tell me they 'hope' they will perform well. Others will tell me they 'think' they'll perform well or that they 'are confident'. Towards the top end of the scale there are a few athletes who 'believe' they will perform well. The ultimate expression of confidence is *knowing*. However, athletes don't always say, 'I know'. Sometimes they say, 'I hope' or 'I believe'. If we look at the range of possible responses, we can see a confidence scale. At the bottom end we could find, 'I hope', and at the top end, 'I know'.

How confident are you that you will perform well?

I hope – I think – I'm confident – I believe – I know

Those who are under-prepared often say, 'I hope'. Those who are well prepared and have the evidence to tell them they can perform will often say, 'I know'. I use this scale with performers in all disciplines. It gives me a starting point for understanding their levels of confidence and allows me to explore the issue further.

A while ago, I was asked to work with an International squash team. As we began the programme, it became obvious that they had an issue when they faced the World Number 1. It was becoming something of a mental block. Our girls didn't really believe that they could beat her. The evidence told them that the World Number 1 had only been beaten once or twice in the previous 2 years. None of our girls had beaten her, even though they'd produced some of their best performances against her. They described the World Number 1 as possessing some very 'hard to beat' qualities. She was physically fast and powerful, and she hit the ball hard. When our girls played a shot that would win against other players, the World Number 1 would return it. They likened the experience to playing against a man.

We needed to give the girls evidence to prove that they could beat the World Number 1. Therefore, we deliberately created situations where our girls faced fast, hard-hitting opponents. We started in the spring, matching the girls against 18–19-year-old elite men. The lads were fast, powerful and hard-hitting. Over a period of 6 months or so, the girls played regularly against fast, powerful players. They naturally started to increase the pace of their game and became accustomed to playing fast-paced opponents. They started to develop tactics and approaches that gave them the upper hand and disarmed their opponent. In the first 'test match' between our girls' team and the elite U19 men, our girls lost 3–0. In the return match (a month or two later), they won. The girls started to develop a game plan that they knew was capable of winning. They also knew that they had developed the skills to execute the game plan. The bank of evidence grew week by week as they started to have more success. By the end of the year, our highest ranked player faced the World Number 1 in the US Open final and beat her.

Here's an important mental note. Many people feel more confident when they have a game plan they believe in and when they know they have the skills to execute it (Australian Institute of Sport, 2010). It makes sense when we consider that 'preparedness' is one of the pillars of confidence (Orlick, 2000).

I was asked to work with a team of senior sales managers in a global financial services corporation a few years ago. My remit was to 'inject belief' into the sales team through the senior managers. During our first workshop together, I asked them to describe their strategy very simply. This was something they really struggled to do. Fundamentally, it seems that their strategy had become over-complicated. Over the years it had evolved and been amended so many times that it became unwieldy. Nobody really understood it, so they didn't have a great deal of faith in it. Step 1 in our task was to produce a strategy (game plan) that everyone had confidence in. The senior management team worked to produce a simple but effective strategy that they had complete belief in and knew they had the ability to deliver. Once we had that, the 'belief' was relatively easy.

How confident would you be if you knew you had a solid game plan and you knew that you had the skills to execute it? How would you feel if you had tried it and tested it in challenging situations and it had given you success? What if it had been successful against tougher challenges than the one you were about to face? I'd guess that you'd *know* you could perform well.

There are some fundamental guidelines that will help to grow confidence:

- Have a great game plan.
- Know the processes you need to deliver.
- Focus on the processes.
- Evaluate the processes.
- Become confident that you can deliver the processes.
- Know that when you deliver the processes, the performance will follow and your chances of achieving the results will be much higher.

'The question that we ask tends to dictate the answer' (Anon) – if we ask 'how confident are you that you will win?' we will get a different answer than if we asked 'how confident are you that you will perform well?'. It's important that we remember our job: What is your 2 Lengths of the pool? We need to get the job right because it will have a knock-on effect on our confidence. If we think our job is to beat the world record holder or win the gold medal, we might not feel particularly confident we can do it. However, if the job is simply to swim 2 Lengths of the pool as fast as we can, the chances are we'll be more confident in our ability to do it. In fact, that example is absolutely true to life. In 2006, Chris (whose job was actually to swim 2 Lengths of the pool as quick as he could) competed in the Commonwealth Games in Melbourne. We had been so focused on his 2 Lengths mantra that it stayed with him in competition. When he took to the blocks for the Commonwealth final he was lined up against seven other competitors. On paper, he was not the fastest swimmer in the race. However, he'd qualified pretty strongly and was swimming well. He had a specific game plan, which he knew and trusted. The game plan was built on hitting a specific stroke rate for the first length, so that he could finish the race strongly. He had practised the race plan and knew he could execute it. For the last few years he'd been completely dedicated to getting his 2 Lengths absolutely right. This focus was so strong that he took it into the race. In the Commonwealth final his job was still to swim 2 Lengths of the pool as fast as he could. The job didn't change just because he happened to be in a major final.

The starter fired the pistol and the swimmers took to the water. Chris managed to execute his first length as per his race plan and turned in fifth place at the half-way mark. Because he managed to deliver the first length as planned, he turned at the wall and knew that he could finish strongly. In the second length he powered through the field and won the race. His job was not to win the gold medal. His job was to swim 2 Lengths of the pool as quickly as he could. Chris did his job. He managed to swim his 2 Lengths quicker than everyone else and therefore won the gold. After the race he was interviewed by Sharron Davies, from the BBC. She asked him how it felt to have won the gold. His answer . . . 'I don't know. I was just swimming 2 Lengths of the pool as quick as I could.'

If that strategy is good enough to win a gold medal, it could well work for you. It applies equally to managing a business, to sales, to education, to medicine or to any other walk of life you care to think of. Gary Dayton (2007) applies the same principles to trading stocks and shares. If we use very basic strategies to control our own confidence, we are likely to perform well in what we do. When we perform well, we are likely to enjoy ourselves. If we're performing well and enjoying ourselves, we're likely to be motivated to keep doing it.

Summary

- Evaluate honestly and objectively.
- Build on what you *can* do.
- Know that you have a great game plan and the knowledge, skill, resources and desire to execute it.
- Remember the simple job and stick to the processes.

5

Master motivation

In psychology, motivation is often known as the 'why of behaviour'. It helps to explain why we do the things we do and even why we don't do the things we should do. There is a reason behind our decisions and our actions, which all stem from our motivation (Rabideau, 2005).

Why does a swimmer get out of bed at 4 am on a cold, wet Tuesday in December to drive all the way to the pool and swim up and down for 2 hours? Why do they then have a bite of breakfast before doing a strength and conditioning session, followed by an hour of physiotherapy, a bite of lunch, a meeting with the performance analyst, a meeting with the coach and back in the pool for another 2 hours? What's it all in aid of? Why do they do all this 6 or 7 days a week for years on end? The answer is perfectly simple for many; it's all in pursuit of an Olympic gold medal. That's what motivates them. That's their reason.

The foundation of motivation is *the reason*. We have to have a reason to do something or a reason not to. Often we forget the importance of this and we do things out of habit. After a while we start to run out of motivation because we have lost sight of the reason. Sportsmen and women fall into this trap frequently. They often start playing sport because it is fun and they simply love doing it. For many, they then start to become successful and their reason starts to change (Deci, Ryan and Koestner, 1999; Jowett and Lavallee, 2007). The sport then becomes a vehicle to achieve success and recognition. Their reason starts to evolve and becomes orientated around winning. A lot of coaches might see this as a good thing. Shouldn't athletes be motivated and driven to win? Isn't that the point? Surely the athletes who are motivated by winning are those who are most likely to be successful. They have a hunger and a desire for success that drives them.

In reality, it can be a double-edged sword. What if the athlete is not experiencing success? What if they are not winning? If their reason for participating is to win, the reason could well disappear. If that happens, motivation will evaporate very quickly. I've known many athletes quit their sport because they hit a tough patch. Their motivation wasn't robust and couldn't carry them through. The irony is that they will say they quit because they weren't enjoying it any more.

Several psychological experiments have shown how motivation can change very quickly (Deci et al., 1999). When children engage in fun tasks, such as drawing, they will often do it simply because they enjoy it. If those children are then given rewards for doing those tasks, they will often choose not to do them if the rewards are taken away. Their motivation changes from engaging in the task simply because they enjoy it, to only engaging in order to receive a reward. In psychological terms, the motivation shifts from being intrinsic (generated from within) to being extrinsic (generated by some external influence). This is the same pattern that is often seen in athletes who shift from participating because they love the sport to participating in order to win and receive recognition (Deci and Ryan, 1985).

I'm sure that you will be able to see the translation into business and everyday life. Let's take another common example. For several years I worked in the health and wellness industry. A lot of my work was geared towards helping people to lose weight and become healthier. As you can imagine, motivation has a massive impact on weight loss. I found that normally the degree of success was dictated by the person's motivation. Unfortunately, many people's motivation was built upon rocky foundations. Their reason for wanting to lose weight was linked to extrinsic factors. Perhaps they wanted to lose weight in order to be more attractive to others. Maybe they wanted other people to notice and comment on how good they looked. Some wanted to fit into smaller clothes so that they would feel better when they compared themselves to other people walking through the shopping centre or in their place of work. Others just needed to see the needle on the scales move so that they could give themselves a pat on the back and know they were being successful at something. All of these motives are extrinsic because they are all dependent upon an outcome. If we are motivated by a result and we don't see the outcome we hope for, we lose the reason for doing it and our motivation evaporates. Imagine a woman who was trying to lose weight so that her friends noticed and complemented her. How would she feel after a month of hard work with no complements? She'd probably say 'what's the point?' and she'd quit because her reason has disappeared.

Of course, there are always a variety of motives that can influence a person (Elliot and Dweck, 2005). It is rare that there is one motive alone. In our weight loss examples, it would be unusual for there to be one reason (i.e. wanting to be complemented). In reality there are probably a number of reasons. However, there will be one or two that are dominant. The same is true within an organization. If we talked to everyone in an office, we'd find a range of motives for each person and therefore a wide variety of motives present within the organization. Why do people engage in their work? Is it for social reasons or because people love being part of a good team? Do they genuinely love the task? Are they motivated by the satisfaction of achieving or winning? Perhaps their motivation is driven by meeting the expectations of their peers or their managers?

The fact is, there are a host of different reasons why people engage in their work (Linder, 1998). In order to understand motivation, we need to start understanding the reasons. This is something that some organizations have already started. A Times 100 (2010) case study shows that the manufacturing giant Siemens has embraced this idea. They realize that their staff are motivated by the challenge of problem solving, the freedom to be creative and use their imagination and the opportunity to experience a variety of stimuli. In fact, Siemens' motivational strategy recognizes that many people are motivated by the prospect of achieving their potential, what Abraham Maslow would call 'self-actualization' (Maslow, 1970, 1998).

All this shows that motivation is a diverse concept. It's not simply a case of waving cash in front of an individual to get more effort from them. It is also important to realize that people's motivation is very rarely 'all or nothing'.

Athletes often find that motivation is enhanced by having a clear focus (Young and Pain, 1999). It's normally easier to focus your mind if there is a big tournament on the horizon. Athletes also tend to be motivated when they are doing well, winning and generally enjoying their game. However, sometimes it is much tougher to motivate yourself. When motivation becomes an issue, athletes often start to take their foot off the gas. They start choosing to do the easier things rather than the difficult things. They don't do quite as many repetitions in the gym or put quite as much effort into their speed sessions. They get despondent quicker. Rather than sticking with a practice until they make it work, they might try it several times but conclude that 'it's just not working, I'll try again tomorrow'. If there is a question as to whether they do a session or postpone, they start choosing to postpone. The end

result is a negative downward spiral of reducing performance, reducing confidence and reducing motivation (Elliot
and Dweck, 2005). If we stop paying attention to our processes, the performance will inevitably drop off. If the
performance drops off, the results will follow.

The same is true outside of sport. People tend not to
approach things as readily if they are not getting the
results. Sales people start to make less sales calls or stop
approaching customers. If managers are having difficulties
in certain departments, they may delegate that responsibility rather than tackle it head on. It's the same reaction
that many of us have to those jobs we really need to do but
that somehow always end up at the bottom of the 'to do list'
and always seem to get put off until tomorrow. The jobs we
put off are rarely the ones we understand and are confident in. More commonly, they are the ones we're not sure
about. We might not have done them before or we might
have struggled with them in the past. These patterns of
deteriorating performance reflect patterns in the negative
performance spirals that we discussed in the opening
chapters (Lindsley et al., 1995).

So, what's the solution? How do we motivate ourselves
consistently throughout all of the ups and down? And how
can we motivate others who are struggling? In order to
have strong motivation, we need a reason that is strong,
robust and compelling. It has to come from within (Deci
and Ryan, 2002). It really is very simple; you have to really
want it. You can't make yourself want something because
someone else wants you to have it. You will never be truly
motivated by the need to please other people. Your motivation has to be genuine and has to come from within. It is
not a coincidence that many truly great people have been
inspired by their dreams. When they are interviewed, they
often talk about the fact that they've been following their
dreams (Torres and Weil, 2009). Many of us don't follow
our dreams. We might think our dreams are silly. We

might not believe they are possible. Our dreams might not fit in with everyone else's expectations or plans for us. We might compromise our dreams for other people.

A friend of mine, who was an aspiring entrepreneur, once said to me 'I don't think I have a dream'. This intrigued me so I started discussing it with him a little more. When we got a little deeper, it became apparent that he had many dreams and ambitions but he'd never given them any real recognition. He'd never seen them as *a dream* because he'd viewed them as a bit outlandish. They weren't very realistic. They were not easily achievable, so he'd assigned them to the junk pile. He hadn't honoured them, recognized them and nurtured them. He'd never given them any energy or worked to try to realize them. Instead, he'd ignored them because he felt they were daft. Ironically, the things he spent his time pursuing were unrelated to his dreams. They were much more realistic but he wasn't genuinely passionate about them. They were a means to an end. Consequently he flitted from one thing to another and never spent very long on any one project. His motivation petered out when he failed to realize the success he was looking for after a few months. Like those trying to lose weight, his motivation was entirely tied to the outcome. If the project didn't make money quickly, there wasn't any point in it. He was not engaged in the project for its own sake or because he believed in it.

I believe that everybody dreams. The difference between those who follow their dreams and those who don't comes down to whether the dreams are honoured, recognized and nurtured. Without recognition and energy, our dreams will wither. If we give them recognition and energy, they will become strong and vibrant (Seligman, 2005).

The simple truth is that if we don't honour our dreams we will never realize them. When we do honour them, believe in them and believe in ourselves, motivation will always be there. Strong motivation will carry us over the hurdles and help us pick ourselves up when we're stuck in a hole. If you have a dream – a compelling reason to do something – your chances of success sky-rocket! If you are doing something purely for an external reason, your motivation will only last as long as the reason remains.

Now all this sounds very idealistic doesn't it. How many people are in a job where they are following their dreams (Linder, 1998)? How many administrators, sales executives or accounts clerks are following their dreams through their careers? Most children aged 6 or 7 years old don't say that they want to be an administrator when they grow up. I'd imagine a typical group of boys would mention the words 'astronaut' or 'footballer' more often than 'recruitment consultant'. So, how can motivation be mastered in situations where we are not absolutely following our heart-felt dreams?

The answer is that we still need a strong and compelling reason (Deci and Ryan, 2002). The activity that we're doing has to mean something to us. It has to be important to us. What benefit is there in doing this job well? What difference would it make if I did it badly? If it's not important to me, there is no reason to do it well (Shah and Gardner, 2008). Why would I invest the time and effort into doing something well if I could invest half as much and just about scrape through?

A few years ago I worked for a Premiership football club. At the time, I saw it as the pinnacle of my career. Many people would probably agree. However, I soon became disillusioned. I had expected that the players would be highly motivated to be the best they could be and to achieve as much as possible for the club. I'll be honest and admit that this was a little naïve. I moved into the football club directly from working in Premiership rugby union. The difference in the motivation of the players was vast. For a while it surprised me. However, the reasons soon became apparent. The footballers were paid tens of thousands of pounds a week. It actually didn't make any significant material difference to them whether they won or lost. The win bonus was tiny in proportion to their basic salary. One morning before a game, I chatted to one of our coaches who'd played the game years before. His basic wage as a player was around £200 per week. The win bonus was also £200 per week. In those days £200 per week bought you a comfortable life with no frills. However, £400 per week bought you a slightly nicer car, a holiday and meals out. Winning made a big difference and consequently the players worked hard. It was similar in the rugby club. Those players who made the England squad had a significantly better lifestyle than those who were squad players in the club. Many of them genuinely aspired to be selected for the International squad because it would make a huge difference to them, both professionally and financially.

There was another fundamental difference between the rugby players and the footballers. In rugby, if you don't work hard in training you could get hurt on the field. In football, it's unlikely that you'll get hurt. You might lose, but that's about the worst that will happen. As a result, the rugby players were motivated to work.

In reality our motivation is not normally purely intrinsic or extrinsic. There is often a combination of motives (Deci and Ryan, 1985). Many of our motives may not be intrinsic initially, but our motivation will become stronger if we can start to create a shift towards intrinsic motives. The fact is, our motivation is usually stronger when we can see a gap between the benefits of doing something and the consequences of not doing it. If we perceive that the gap is large, we tend to be more motivated. If we perceive it to be small, we tend to be less motivated.

Let's take an everyday example. A few chapters ago I mentioned working in a café restaurant business. Our aim was to produce world class cuisine, with world class service. World class for us meant being the best in our sector. We were not a Michelin-starred restaurant. We were in the leisure dining sector, with the likes of Pizza Express and Frankie & Benny's. Therefore, world class service didn't mean silver service. Our food wasn't gourmet, but it did have to be the best in our sector. Our challenge was to achieve this standard with our team.

Like many businesses, we were quite picky in our selection process. We spent a great deal of time ensuring we had good people in the first place. The fact that we had a fairly intense selection process helped our staff to understand that we were serious about providing a world class product. In our business, most of the team were either kitchen staff or service staff. In order to ensure that they delivered the greatest possible output, we created an environment that would motivate them to be the best they could be. Firstly, we ensured that our basic rate of pay was slightly higher than that of our competitors. As a result, staff wanted to work for us. We also put a multi-dimensional incentive package in place, which allowed the staff to benefit when they produced a high standard. We ensured that our incentives ranged from recognition through to rewards. Sometimes, a simple 'well done' or a pat on the back is incredibly motivating for someone. However, we also knew that prizes and cash bonuses did motivate the team. We created a range of incentives that allowed us to give very immediate rewards (on a daily basis) as well as rewards for monthly, quarterly and annual performance. Finally, we structured our incentive programme to reward the individuals, the teams (i.e. shift teams) and also the staff as a whole when they achieved their targets.

At the other end of the scale, we had very strict standards of conduct and professionalism that were written into the job descriptions and working policies. The bottom line was that if a member of staff didn't conform to these, they would not remain on the team. These standards were higher than those of our competitors, and so was our basic rate of pay. If any member of the team didn't want to deliver our standards they were very welcome to work for someone else, which probably meant taking a pay cut.

This two-pronged strategy created quite a wide gap. There was a very real reason for our team to perform at their best. There was a tangible difference between doing their best when they came to work and just getting to the end of the shift. On any given shift, the team could be subject to a mystery-shopper visit. If the team achieved an 8/10 or better in every category of their mystery-shopper assessment, each member would receive a bonus. The team didn't know which shift would have the mystery-shopper visit, so they needed to be on their toes at all times. In addition, the shift leaders would set targets for the team during each shift, with a slightly different emphasis for each member. Importantly, these would be followed up and evaluated so that staff knew that their performance mattered and was recognized. Our MVP (Most Valued Player) award each month was given to the team member who'd contributed the most to the team. We worked hard to ensure that the prize for the MVP was always very personal for the winner. Our very first MVP spent much of his spare time coaching his son, who was a talented young footballer. Knowing this, we chose his MVP prize carefully. We opted for a soccer coaching pack including DVDs, books and a ball. We also managed to secure a pair of tickets for our MVP and his son to watch their team. Although it required some effort to pull the prize together, it meant a tremendous amount to him and had far more value than it cost us. It showed the rest of the team that the MVP prize was worth working for, and also showed that we genuinely took an interest in them as people.

I know this is all very small scale. We are not talking about mega bonuses for investment bankers, but it shows that by understanding some basic principles and managing the motivational environment it is possible to achieve fantastic performances from a team. The absolute foundation of motivation, as we've already discovered, is *the reason*.

Managers and coaches can sometimes assume that their team knows *the reason*. At times we can take it for granted that we're all on the same page when, in reality, we may not be. I have made that mistake myself. When working in Premiership football, I was often frustrated when players didn't apply themselves fully to some of the work we were doing. When I reflected on it, there was a possibility that the players didn't really understand why that particular session was important. I assumed that it was perfectly obvious, when in fact it may not have been obvious to the players. As a result, I started to change my approach slightly when I began working for a Championship club in the following season. At the start of every session I would take one minute to explain the session to the players and the reason we were doing it (I called it my 'Magic One Minute'). I made a point to always let the players know why the session was important and how it contributed to their performance on the field. Unsurprisingly, that one minute proved to be incredibly valuable and the quality and effort from the players increased dramatically.

As a sport psychologist, I've worked with a lot of athletes and their coaches. One athlete–coach pairing worked together for years (Hartley, 2007). They spent 4 or 5 hours a day in each other's company for 6 days a week, as well as travelling to competitions together. Their relationship was very solid and open. However, one day I challenged them to each complete a performance profile on the athlete. The performance profile is a fairly simple exercise (Horn, 2008). The first job is to identify the key elements of the athlete's performance (i.e. the *5 Keys to Success* that we discussed in Chapter 2). In a performance profile, we might include as many as eight things rather than five, but the process is the same. Once we have identified the key elements we apply a score (0–10), which provides a rating of the athlete's current ability in that element. When we have a score for each, we set a target for each area and establish a set of priorities. For example, a swimmer might rate his starts as 3/10 and set a target level of 6/10 before the next major competition. Of course, the time available will often dictate how much improvement we can reasonably target. If we only have a few weeks, the improvement possible might only be one or two points. As we look at the elements, we may also identify that starts are a priority area because they will give us the greatest performance gain. At the end of the exercise the athlete and the coach will have independently produced a performance profile each. It will identify the key areas, the current level of ability (as each of them sees it), the target and the priority areas.

Now you'd probably have expected the coach and the athlete to produce fairly similar profiles. For a start you'd expect them to identify the same key elements. You'd probably also expect them to have a similar view of the athlete's current ability in each area and would reasonably expect them to have similar priorities. After all, they are working on the same performance and they spend many, many hours together doing it. In reality though, the profiles were vastly different. The key elements were very different. The coach and the athlete had actually only identified one or two of the same elements from a list of eight. Of the elements that they did agree on, the scoring was vastly different. On one element the athlete scored himself as 3/10 and the coach scored him as 8/10. Of course, this meant that their priority areas for training were also very different. As you can imagine, this has a knock-on effect. The coach is setting a training programme that he believes will target the key elements and the major priorities for the athlete. However, the athlete thinks that he needs to work on an entirely different set of skills. How motivated do you think the athlete will be when he picks up the training card? Will he look at it and immediately know the reason for each of the exercises and understand exactly how those exercises will improve his performance? No, probably not. As a consequence, it is unlikely that he will pull out all the stops and focus 100 per cent on delivering the best training session possible. The athlete is more likely to complete the session without pushing himself to the limit or absolutely honing in on the finer details. At the very highest level, it is the tiny details that make all the difference (Hartley, 2007).

Simply having a clear focus in itself tends to be highly motivating (Young and Pain, 1999; Orlick, 2000). You probably already experience this yourself. Some days you will get up and know exactly what you have to do. Your schedule will be set and you'll probably have some very clear goals or outcomes for your day. Other days you may get up and start to think about the day ahead. It might not be very structured. You may start the day wondering exactly what you're going to be doing. Many people will find that when they have a very clear focus it is easier to be motivated. If we're not as sure what we're doing, then it's often harder to get motivated. The Times 100 (2010) case study with Siemens also identifies that focus, in itself, enhances motivation. The study identifies that Siemens deliberately create very specialist roles with tight defini-tion as part of their wider motivational strategy. It all links back to our need for a *reason* to engage in something. If we have a clear focus, we have *the reason*, which fuels our motivation. Without that clear focus, we might be struggling to find our *reason*.

Motivation is not an island. It is not an isolated element of psychology. As with everything else, it is integrally linked with both focus and confidence (Bandura, 1997; Orlick, 2000; Elliot and Dweck, 2005). When we have focus and confidence, it is likely that our motivation will be higher. Incentives are useful but can pull us away from our intrinsic motives (Deci and Ryan, 2002). However, incentives only tend to work if we have the belief that we can accomplish the task in the first place. Often motivation, confidence and focus are dampened when we perceive that we're under pressure (Weinberg and Gould, 2010).

Summary

- Know the reason.
- Know why you're doing the task and the importance of doing it well.
- If your reasons have an intrinsic value, they are more likely to be robust and enduring.
- Have a clear focus. A performance profile can be a great tool to do this.
- Honour your dreams!

6

Deconstructing pressure

> Pressure is a word that is misused in our vocabulary. When you start thinking of pressure, it's because you've started to think of failure.
>
> (Tommy Lasorda, LA Dodgers Coach)

There is no such thing as pressure. This might seem like a sensationalist statement designed to catch your attention, but actually when you read on you find out it's not quite what it seems. I assure you that the statement is very straightforward and is absolutely true. It is one of the great secrets in sport psychology that even the professionals often get wrong. Most sport psychologists and coaches talk about 'managing pressure', which makes the mistake of assuming that it exists.

I view the concept of 'dealing with pressure' in the same way I'd view arguing with an imaginary friend. Have you ever tried to win an argument against an imaginary friend? It's almost impossible. You cannot win. Before you've even finished making your point, you have already retorted with a counter-argument. It's a futile exercise. To be honest, it's pretty pointless too. Who cares if you win the argument? The other party is imaginary. The only way to resolve the situation is to refuse to engage in the argument in the first place because it isn't real. It's the same with pressure. It doesn't exist, so managing it is a nonsense. In fact, by trying to manage it we start to believe it might be real (just like the imaginary friend we're arguing with). 'Pressure is nothing more than the shadow of great opportunity' (Michael Johnson).

Let's start with the basics. People create pressure for themselves (Beilock, 2010). The only way we can ever experience 'pressure' is to create it in our own minds. It is a product of our imagination. If we experience 'pressure' it is because we are projecting an imaginary view of the future (Markman, Klein and Suhr, 2008). We use our imagination when we create images and pictures, narratives, fantasies, thought-flows and so on (Markman et al., 2008). Often, we start imagining what might happen if we don't achieve the outcome we desire. 'What if I don't win?' . . . 'What will the press say?' . . . 'What will the coach say?' . . . 'What will people think?' . . .

By projecting forward an image of what might happen, we may start doubting the outcome and feeling uneasy. We need to recognize that our imagination is incredibly powerful. Used positively it can help us to optimize our performance. However, we have to be aware that we also use our imagination to create trapdoors for ourselves.

Even if we think other people are putting pressure on us, we must recognize that ultimately we are the only ones capable of creating pressure (Najemy, 2002). Often people experience pressure if they perceive that they need to meet certain expectations, or perceive that a bad performance may meet with negative evaluation from other people (Dunn, 1999; Dunn and Syrotuik, 2003). This phenomenon has also been seen outside of sport, in fields such as performing arts (Sutcliffe, 1997; Harlow, 1999). It is probably something you've experienced yourself at some point in your life. However, expectations, or negative evaluations, don't automatically lead to 'pressure'.

If other people have an expectation of us, it is actually our choice whether we accept that expectation or not (Valle and Halling, 1989; Glasser, 1999). If I said to you that I expected you to become the World Number One tennis player in the next 12 months, you would probably ignore my expectation. You'd think I was completely mad and you'd bin my expectation. You'd choose not to accept it. You can do exactly the same if a manager, coach, teammate, parent, partner or anyone else tells you they have an expectation of you. We often tend to accept an expectation from someone close to us without questioning it. This is especially true if that person's expectation matches one that we have for ourselves. If your manager tells you that they expect you to hit a certain target, and you agree with them, it's likely that you'd adopt that expectation and use it as a target for yourself.

Like pressure, expectations are also figments of our imagination. They are imaginary projections into the future. Any view of the future must be produced in our imagination because there is nowhere else it can come from (Markman et al., 2008). Expectations could be a product of either your imagination or someone else's. The point is, expectations are not real. They are conjured up in our imagination and in the imagination of other people. It's not wise to let our own imagination dictate our thoughts and feelings. However, it is even less wise to let someone else take control of them. Do you really want your thoughts and emotions to be dictated by someone else's imaginary projections? That's a bit like giving them a remote control for your thoughts and feelings.

It doesn't matter what anyone else expects. Their expectation is irrelevant *because* it comes from their imagination. I'm not trying to be cruel. The simple principle is that we should only concern ourselves with reality, not fantasy. Fantasy is a product of our imagination, just as expectations and pressure are (Markman et al., 2008). Often people have hopes for us, which they express. We sometimes take those on board as expectations, which we then try to fulfil. If we buy into expectations, we are trying to live up to a fantasy. The best thing to do is to recognize it for what it is and get on with reality.

Here is an excerpt from a session with an elite junior racket sport player:

> We chatted about how we can construct and also de-construct pressure. As we said, if we experience pressure it is because we create it. We are the only ones who can ever put pressure on ourselves. We talked about how this worked. When you are thinking about the British Championships, you could create pressure for yourself by thinking . . . 'I'm number 1', 'I'm meant to win', 'what if I don't?', 'what will people think?', 'I expect myself to win', 'I want to win', 'I want my name in lights', etc.
>
> If you think this way, you create this imaginary, illusionary pressure on yourself. However, it doesn't have to be that way. You could choose to de-construct it. During the session you did a really good job of explaining to me why there was no pressure, namely because you can't change or control anyone else's expectations. If you don't win then you don't win. If you give it your best, you've done all you can do. It is fine to want to win but it is pointless expecting it.
>
> It is important to remember the job that you have to do. You do not have to win (that's not the job) or be number 1 (that's not it either). Your only job is to play the best you can on the day – that's it – nothing else!
>
> Remember, you choose the expectations that you accept. If I expect you to become senior England captain next week you can choose to ignore that expectation. You can do the same when someone says 'you should beat her'. It doesn't matter if they think that. It's completely irrelevant.

Athletes feel 'pressure' when they get *the job* wrong (Lane, 2001). Typically, athletes think that their job is to win, to climb up the rankings and to secure prize money or sponsorship. Sales people think that *the job* is to hit their sales target. However, none of those things is *the job*. Normally when we get the job wrong it is because we're too busy focusing on the outcome. Our job is to deliver the process. That is the bit we can control. Our job is not to achieve an outcome. At this point I can see some thought bubbles appearing. Do I really mean that the job is not to achieve an outcome? Surely that is a cop-out. Aren't we all in the results business? Most of the football managers, head coaches and performance directors I've known would certainly say they were in the results business. That also goes for sales directors, managing directors, chief executives, school principals and just about anyone else. Of course there is an outcome that we're working towards, but our focus should not be tied to it. If we focus on the result, we will often forget the process. Many people focus on the result, rather than delivering the processes that would give them the best chance of achieving it. So many people put energy into worrying about what will happen if they don't hit the target that they forget to focus on doing what they need to do (Rotella, 2004). We spend so much time worrying about the things we can't control, and too little focusing on the things we can control.

By aiming for the result, we set ourselves a job that is outside of our control (Bull, 1996). The fact that it is outside of our control means that it's uncertain. Winning is never certain. Hitting a target is never certain. There is always an element of uncertainty. This uncertainty is what tends to cause us the angst (Boelen and Reijntjes, 2009). How can we be completely confident in our ability to achieve something that has uncertainty? If you're trying to do an 'impossible' job or even a job that you have no control over, you will probably imagine pressure because you will not be 100 per cent sure that you can do the job. The job might seem too big. If the job is to win the tournament, an athlete might doubt their ability to do that. Even a confident athlete won't *know* that they can do that job. There is often a gap between what we believe we can achieve and what we think we must achieve. That gap manifests as the worry and anxiety we associate with pressure. This is illustrated in Csikszentmihalyi's (2008) model of the challenge and skills balance (see Figure 3.1 on page 46). If we create an expectation for ourselves, we post a target. If we are not absolutely sure that we can achieve that target, we might start to have doubts and worries. If we also give that target some meaning, we will magnify our doubts and worries.

Here is a piece from a report that I wrote for an elite junior golfer after our first session together. The golfer was exceptionally talented but produced Jekyll and Hyde performances. He would play extremely well when there was 'no pressure' and was a wreck when 'under pressure'.

We kicked off by talking about the difference between your round on Saturday (an impressive score of 68) and your round on Sunday (which you weren't happy with). The round on Saturday was a small internal club competition, whereas Sunday's was a County event. You described Saturday's experience by saying that it was like watching yourself from your living room. The shots seemed to almost play themselves. You likened it to playing a shot where someone pressed the 'save' button. After that it's as if someone pressed 'play' and the shots just kept coming out almost automatically and near-perfectly. You weren't thinking about your shots, you were just playing naturally and enjoying yourself. On Sunday (just 24 hours later) your performance nose dived. You said you were anxious and felt under pressure. You didn't start particularly well but once you'd made a couple of slight errors, these compounded and the errors started to get bigger and more frequent. You said your game 'fell apart'.

We talked about the difference between the two events. You said that Saturday's game was on your home course. You knew the other competitors and you knew you could beat them. You also said that there was no pressure because it wasn't an important competition. On Sunday there was a trophy at the end of the competition and you perceived it as being more important. You were playing on a course you'd only played a handful of times and you didn't know who you were competing against. In reality there is no real difference between the two matches. Your job is the same for each match. You simply have to play the best game of golf you can. You know what you need to do to play good shots. It doesn't matter where you play. Your challenge is simply to play the best shot you can when you get to the ball. It doesn't matter what name they put on the trophy. It doesn't matter whether you're playing Tiger Woods or me. Your job is not to beat the opponent. If you played Tiger and got round in 60 shots and lost, would that be acceptable? If you played me and got round in 80 shots, but won, would that be acceptable?

We spent a while discussing the reason why winning has been so important to you. This led us on to talking about your dreams of becoming a pro on the circuit. When we discussed this in more depth, you also started talking about wanting the other people to notice how good you are. We chatted about wanting to be successful and almost escape the prospect of a mediocre life, working for 30 years in a factory. You know that you're talented, and I also know you get frustrated when you don't show the world how talented you are. I sense that if you didn't become a pro on the circuit, you'd kick yourself because you'd feel like you'd not made the most of your talent.

There are lots of potential trapdoors here. Wanting to become a pro is fine, but at the moment it is turning a simple shot into a life-and-death event. If you're not careful, the shot becomes a judgement of how good you are and how successful you are. It also becomes an indicator of whether you can achieve your dreams and escape the prospect of leading an average life. It tells you whether you're doomed to work in the same factory for 30 years or if you can live your dreams. Your imagination starts to create a lot of baggage around the shot, which your mind then turns into pressure. As you now know, pressure doesn't actually exist.

We talked about the danger that golf becomes like a really narrow pinnacle. If you believe that your life depends on being successful in golf, shots start to become a bit like facing a firing squad. If failing at golf means failing as a person, there is a lot to lose if you mess up a shot. You said that losing £15,000 would be a lot of money to you. We talked about the 'pressure' you might feel if you were faced with a 3 foot putt that would potentially win or lose you £15,000. If £15,000 was a lot to lose by missing a 3 foot putt, compare that to the prospect of losing your hopes and dreams. That is why being successful in life cannot hinge on your performance on the golf course. The trick is to be happy with your life right now. Have a good job, run a car, be able to take care of yourself, be good at what you do. These are the things that you said are important to you right now, therefore they need to be firmly in place. If you know that you can be a success whether you sink the putt or miss it, you're more likely to see it as a simple shot and not a life-and-death situation.

We talked about the difference between a 3 foot putt played on your home course when you are out practising by yourself and a 3 foot putt at Augusta in a competition with a title, prize money and a television audience of millions. The obvious point is that there is no difference . . . unless your mind makes it different.

This principle applies not only to golf shots and putting. It is equally true for a sale, a deal, an interview, an exam or anything else that we feel has pressure. It is very rare that we are actually in a life-and-death situation, although sometimes we give situations that meaning (Frankl, 1959/ 1984). If you have ever watched talent shows on TV (e.g. *X Factor*), you will see contestants who are incredibly nervous before a performance. The reason they are nervous is because they have decided to pin all of their hopes and dreams onto singing a song. Some of them perceive that the success of their life depends on a judge saying 'yes' or 'no'. In their mind, a 'yes' keeps the hope of stardom alive and a 'no' means that their dreams of leading a successful life are over. It would be a different story if they were already happy with their life and saw the prospects that they had beyond singing. If singing, golf or any other task becomes 'all or nothing', we're likely to create a very strong illusion of pressure that could consume us.

To help us ensure that we get *the job* right, we need to make sure we don't start attaching meanings to our performance. Sometimes this happens because we take on the hopes and expectations of others. International players often feel that they carry 'the hopes of the nation'. Some teams and individuals habitually under-perform when they reach the major world events. The reason for this may well be because the athletes feel pressure to perform for their nation (Gerrard, 2010). For example, when athletes compete for their country, in their national sport, there is normally a lot of media hype. This is true in New Zealand for the All Blacks and in England for the England Football Team.

I spoke to a friend of mine on this very subject. My friend has worked in elite sport for years at professional club level and international level. He is a New Zealander. Our conversation focused on the reasons why the All Blacks often fail to deliver in the Rugby Union World Cup (Huw, 2010). I suggested that the players might struggle with the pressure that they perceive when they represent New Zealand in the World Cup. They might perceive that their nation's hopes ride with them. There is a great mystique and prestige in 'the All Black shirt'. In my opinion this could well be a part of the issue. Maybe the All Black players see the shirt as something more than just a shirt. In reality it is simply some material that has been stitched together. In my friend's opinion, it is legendary. It carries a history and a legacy. If that's how the players see it, then maybe they don't simply view the game for what it is. Is a rugby match just a game between 30 players, with one ball, a pitch with a set of white lines, some posts at either end and some officials? In my eyes, that is exactly what it is. In the eyes of the players, maybe it's a chance to realize or break the hopes of millions of people. Maybe it's the chance to achieve their lifelong ambitions and become a legend in their country. Perhaps it's a chance to secure their financial future for life. If it becomes anything more than just a game between 30 players on a 70 m × 100 m rectangle of grass, then we've started to enter the world of fantasy and imagination. If we start buying into anything outside of that, we are making a departure from what's real and starting to focus on the illusions.

Perhaps the same could be said for the England Football team. In the 2010 World Cup hosted by South Africa, England performed well below par. There were several possible reasons given for the performances. On a number of occasions the England manager cited 'fear' and 'pressure' (Christenson, 2010). Many people would logically deduce that this was linked closely to the media coverage and the hype that had been created in the lead-up to the event. However, the media coverage and the hype will only be perceived as 'pressure' if we buy into it. Just like any other expectation, it's borne out of the imagination. Anything that is future orientated must come from our imagination because it hasn't happened yet. The only place it can come from is our imagination. In this case, it was the imaginations of the journalists, the public, The Football Association, the sponsors and possibly even the players and staff of Team England. However, there may well have been an extra dimension.

Normally the issue becomes further exacerbated when our ego becomes involved (Metzinger, 2010). It's possible that the England players bought into the media hype because they have tied themselves so closely to the media. The media is the vehicle that provides them with a public image and a public profile. Without that public image and profile, they would not be paid tens (or hundreds) of thousands of pounds every week to kick footballs around. If it wasn't for the media's insatiable appetite for football, the players would not be household names. So, there is far more likelihood that the players will care about what the media says and how they are portrayed. Their image and their profile become paramount. All of a sudden the game is more than just 22 blokes playing on a grass pitch with a ball, two goals and a trio of officials. It becomes an exercise in making sure that the papers stay on side and the nation is behind them. The players are likely to focus on the sizeable difference between doing well, along with the media benefits this brings, and doing badly where the negative media coverage has a knock-on effect on the players' lives. If this happens, the chances are that the players will get *the job* wrong. They might start thinking that their job is to impress the papers or protect their image. They may perceive a 'need to win' so that they can save face and be portrayed well. Perhaps they become focused on the need to become a hero, or to avoid becoming a villain, rather than focusing on playing football. They will probably project forwards an image of a future where they have performed badly, they have been knocked out and have returned home under a cloud of criticism. This is a future most English players would want to avoid.

Consequently, the tendency would be to worry about what would happen if that future became reality – and so the illusion of pressure is borne in their minds.

When the game becomes more than just the game, then we have got the game wrong. When a tennis match become more than just a game between two players with rackets, a ball, a net and some white lines, then we're not playing tennis any more. If the game becomes a chance to impress someone, a means of getting recognition or a way of paying back the parents who have spent a fortune so far, then it's not a game of tennis any more. Instead, we are playing a game we have absolutely no control over. We cannot control whether someone else is impressed with us. We cannot control whether someone gives us recognition. It is not our job to pay our parents back through our performances. If parents choose to support our sport, their choice should be made purely because they love to support us in whatever we do. It should not be dependent on our performance, winning, ranking or title. None of those things is our job.

As we've said already, we create pressure and therefore we can 'de-construct it' (Manz, 2000). The easiest way is not to create it in the first place. However, if we do feel pressure, we have the ability to dismantle it and start to see the reality rather than the illusion. One of the best ways to do this is to simply find all the reasons why there is no pressure in a situation. If you start to perceive pressure, take a few moments to remind yourself why there is no pressure and never was any pressure. Normally this involves a slight reality check and a quick reminder of the job. Once we do that, we are more likely to be able to focus on exactly what we need to do in that moment. In reality the job we need to do will normally be pretty simple and something we're very capable of doing. Rather than trying to 'serve for the match' or 'win Championship point', we'll simply be trying to serve. Instead of trying to win the World Cup, the job is simply to take a penalty kick. Rather than attempting to win the Ryder Cup, the job is simply to execute a 3 foot putt (Fisher, 1998).

When working with an International squash team, I often heard them referring to 'big points'. Of course, I understood what they were referring to, but I asked them how many points a *big point* was worth. Is it worth three points, or five or ten? Naturally the answer was that the big points are worth one point, the same as all the others. However, because the players perceived them differently, they played them differently. *Match point* is a classic example. Instead of doing the very good things that got them to match point against the World Number 1, they would change and try something completely different. They would force a shot that wasn't really on. Their patience would all of a sudden desert them and they'd try to play a winner too early. So often they would end up losing by the odd point because they started to play differently right at the end. They started to perceive pressure in the *big points*. Interestingly, this pattern happened in *big events*, against *big opponents* or in *big points*. Rather than simply playing the ball and playing the point in front of them, they started to inject a different meaning to it all. When they started to accept that every point was equal, and that the competition or the opponent was irrelevant, they were able to play their shots more naturally. When they ditched the mental baggage, they began to play each point on its own merit and play one point at a time.

Once performers have got the hang of de-constructing pressure, I like to start stress testing it with them to see how robust it is. Like many things, it's easy to ditch pressure in a classroom environment or a training session. It's a greater challenge in the heat of competition. To put it into a practical setting, I often use 'pressure training' exercises (Taylor and Wilson, 2005). In reality that is probably a daft name. The aim of 'pressure training' is simple. The performer's task is simply to stick to their job, even though we may throw things at them to tempt them away. I work with the coach to create a set of scenarios and challenges that tempt the performer out of sticking to their simple job. Some refer to this as mental toughness (Jones, Hanton and Connaughton, 2007).

Let's look at an example of pressure training with the elite junior golfer who produced the Jeckle and Hyde performances. We started on the putting green. Once we had identified some simple things to focus on, he set about putting. He took some shots from various distances and from different positions on the green, sinking 8/10. I then added a simple challenge. If he scored eight in his next 10 shots, his Dad would buy him a CD. If he scored less than six, he had to wash his Dad's car. The golfer's challenge was simple. He just had to keep playing the shots as he did before I introduced the challenge. This principle is one that can be applied very easily to a host of different situations. The introduction of competition is a simple challenge, that tempts many to start playing differently. Introducing competition with a reward for winners and a consequence for losers often adds to the challenge. With an International archery squad, the losers were required to clear up, carry the bags and do the chores for the winners. Even simple things like asking players to put £20 into an envelope, which will be the prize for the winner, adds a dimension. However, there are other things that often cause people to forget the simple job. Those who like structure can often get flustered if their routine is broken or their preparation is interrupted. The job is to perform at your best. Sometimes things happen that will disrupt preparations and routines. However, the job is still to do the best you can and focus on delivering the performance. For people who live for positive feedback from others, generating a negative atmosphere can draw them away from doing the simple job. The job was never to please other people or to elicit positive feedback. The job has always been to perform as well as you can.

Therefore, providing negative feedback is often a real test. All of the scenarios that we present are designed to test how robustly a performer can stick to the simple job. If negative feedback from their coach has an effect on their performance, it is because they are still trying to impress the coach. If losing has an effect, it is because they still believe the job is to win.

The same exercises can be done in a business environment, an educational environment or any other environment you can imagine. Many reality TV shows are examples of the same thing. *The Apprentice*, broadcast by the BBC, is a prime example. A group of people are given a task to do with a set of conditions imposed. There is a competitive element, a big prize at the end and the added spice of having millions of viewers to impress. This all creates the illusion of pressure. In many reality TV shows, the competitors are also often sleep deprived, hungry and thirsty so as to increase the chances of creating the emotional outbursts that make for good television.

The basis of *pressure training* is the same as any other form of training. In order to get better, we need a challenge that is slightly beyond our current capabilities. It is the same principle that we employ when we're trying to get fit. You can't expect to get fitter by running the same distance at the same speed. We won't increase our ability simply by doing the same things in the same way. At best you'll maintain your fitness, but you won't increase it. To increase, your body needs a greater stimulus. To develop, we need to push our boundaries and step outside of our comfort zone.

Summary

- Pressure is a product of our imagination.
- We normally experience pressure when we attach meanings to the performance and focus on the outcome.
- Pressure is exacerbated when our ego gets involved.
- De-construct pressure by seeing the job for what it really is.
- Put your mind to the test. Try stress testing to see how robust it is.

7

Love your discomfort zone

Most of us like to operate in our comfort zone. By definition, our comfort zone encompasses those things that we're familiar with, those things that we know and are confident in (Bardwick, 1995; Cotterill and Johnson, 2008; White, 2009). In fact, Alistair White (2009) refers to it as a state in which a person operates in an 'anxiety-neutral condition', using a limited set of skills to deliver steady performance, normally with low risk. Tasks that fall into our comfort zone are those that we are competent at and find relatively easy. We don't tend to find these sorts of tasks terribly demanding or challenging. The situations that would fall into our comfort zone are those in which we are confident operating in. It is possible that we can engage in a task that we'd consider to be well within our comfort zone, but in a situation that lies outside of it. For example, a rugby goal-kicker might be taking a regulation kick on a poor surface, with a crosswind and driving rain. The task is not particularly demanding but the situation pushes the performer into their discomfort zone.

Although our comfort zone is quite a cozy place to be, in many ways it's also a dangerous place to be (Bardwick, 1995). We don't tend to develop or improve when we operate in our comfort zone. We do not tend to learn very much in our comfort zone. Geoff Colvin (2008) notes that to excel in any field we need to engage in a great deal of *deliberate practice*. In fact, *deliberate practice* is seen by many to be the foundation for expertise and exceptional performance

(Ericsson and Charness, 1999). Interestingly, Geoff Colvin notes that *deliberate practice* is often uncomfortable, which is why not many people do it and why not many people truly excel in what they do.

Many people believe that we would become more confident by doing tasks we're comfortable and familiar with. However, our confidence becomes limited to those things that are within our comfort zone. Our tendency often is to restrict ourselves to doing those things we are comfortable with and we start to shy away from things that would push us into uncharted territories. In a sense, we create a more solid wall around our comfort zone, which starts to act as a barrier, stopping us from attempting new challenges. We start to believe that if we can't do something right now we won't be able to do it, and so we don't even attempt it. This is one of the strongest reasons for regularly operating in your discomfort zone and always challenging yourself to push the envelope. The evidence will tell you that you can take on new challenges and become good at things you've never tried before.

We grow when we enter our discomfort zone. By consistently exposing ourselves to challenges and demands, we develop and learn. In fact, our comfort zone gradually expands to include the new challenges. As we become more familiar with the demands and become more competent in them, those situations and tasks become comfortable. Let's look at some simple examples:

- *Example 1.* In Chapter 4 we looked at the strategy that we employed with the squash girls. The programme deliberately took them outside of their comfort zone and challenged them in new ways. Pitching them against faster, more powerful and harder hitting opponents was definitely uncomfortable for them. Before engaging in the programme, it was something they avoided doing. However, there was another dimension to the discomfort zone that we created. A few months previously, the girls had struggled to perform in a World Team Championship event. They were odds on favourites to win on paper, but they ended up losing the final to the host team in front of their home fans. When I spoke to the girls, they started talking about the pressure of the event and how the media and supporters in the UK expected them to win. Knowing this, we made sure that the test matches that we set up for the girls were all covered in the squash media. We created some media hype around the matches. This all served to create a multi-dimensional challenge to the players. Gradually their comfort zone grew to encompass the things they were previously uncomfortable with. The result was that the girls won the European Team tournament comfortably and our top player beat the 'fast, powerful and hard hitting' World Number 1 in the following autumn.

- *Example 2.* I worked for several years in Premiership Rugby Union. One year I watched one of our players at work. He is a very good professional and works extremely hard on his game. One of the key facets of his game is kicking. I used to watch his kicking sessions with great interest. The player would consistently set himself difficult challenges that were well outside of his comfort zone. He would often aim at a very small target and challenge himself to hit the target repeatedly. For example, he may aim at a single post from 20 metres and challenge himself to hit it 10 times in a row. If he hit nine but missed the tenth, he'd go back and start again from zero. Once he'd done 10, he would increase the challenge. He might increase the distance or work against a cross-wind to make it harder. It would be the same if he was kicking out of hand. As the practice progressed, he would increase his precision and accuracy, or have players charge at him to reduce his time and space. I started to realize that the player was actively using his discomfort zone to make him a better player. Whenever a practice became comfortable, he'd change it to make it uncomfortable again. As a result he became a better player. He was able to produce difficult skills, executed precisely, with very little time or space.

- *Example 3*. I actively encourage people to understand their comfort zone and their discomfort zone, and to seek out opportunities to enter their discomfort zone. A swimmer who I worked with for many years became very adept at doing this. On one occasion he entered a competition in Eastern Europe because he knew it would be challenging and uncomfortable. He knew that getting there would be reasonably difficult because it was off the beaten track. He knew that the accommodation would be far from luxurious, the food would be basic and the pool would be cold. Importantly, he also knew that the competition would be dominated by young, keen and talented Eastern Europeans who were all competing on their own doorsteps. The opposition would all be in race condition (rested, tapered and shaved), because this was one of their big events of the year. In comparison, our swimmer knew that he was in the middle of a heavy training phase and was fatigued. Many athletes would probably have entered the competition with their excuses already lined up. However, his job was to go and perform at his best, even though many of the conditions were against him. One of the aims of the exercise was to deliberately put him in a situation that exposed any cracks in his performance. We needed to see any potential weaknesses so that we could work on them and strengthen them.

He also selected meets in which he would face some of his major opponents in Europe, and the World, head to head. Rather than choosing opportunities that would give him the best chance of beating them, he chose times when the odds were against him. On one occasion, he competed in the middle of a very heavy block of training. I remember the athlete telling me that he was stiff and sore as he stood on the blocks ready to start the race. In comparison, his main opponent was race ready. Despite this, he finished a very close second and only slightly outside of his personal best. These experiences also taught him that he could perform in tough situations. He could produce a swim just outside of his personal best when he was tired and sore. He didn't need absolutely perfect preparation in order to swim fast. If his preparation was thrown out for some reason, or he didn't physically feel on top of the world, he knew that he could pull out a good time anyway. That knowledge only came because he deliberately stepped into his discomfort zone. He sought to become comfortable with those things he was unsure about or uncomfortable with.

Of course, there are many parallels outside of sport. Business people and entrepreneurs often do the same. It's also true of surgeons, teachers, musicians, traders (Wolfinger, 2008) and people in many other walks of life. They take on new challenges, they innovate, they push the envelope. The world of business is incredibly dynamic, as is medicine, education, science, the performing arts and every other field you care to think of. As a human race, if we didn't step into our discomfort zone, we would never have discovered anything. Explorers would never have charted the Earth. Technologists would never have invented the microchip. NASA would never have launched anything into space. On a much more personal level, peak performances occur when we operate on the edge of our capability (Csikszentmihalyi, 1990). These innovations are not a product of the comfort zone; they are a product of the discomfort zone.

I come across a common challenge for executives and managers in business environments. Many of them have similar discomfort zones. They tend to feel comfortable when they feel in control. However, this can become dysfunctional when they are managing other people. The challenge for many is to relinquish control and allow others to take control in certain situations. This requires a great deal of trust. I notice that this is particularly common in business owners or chief executive officers (Aronoff, 2011). Much of my work with executives revolves around helping them enter this discomfort zone. Initially, they don't see it as part of their discomfort zone, because it doesn't involve working harder, working longer or increasing their targets. When we stop and look at it though, the reality becomes obvious. Relinquishing control is clearly in their discomfort zone because they are uncomfortable with the prospect and they typically find it so hard to do.

So why don't we all habitually launch into our discomfort zones? There are several potential reasons. Some people might see this as risk taking. Some people initially don't like the sensation of being uncomfortable. When we enter the discomfort zone, we often encounter uncertainty and a loss of control. I know from personal experience that sometimes the discomfort zone can be an almost scary place. I often step a long way into my discomfort zone, sometimes beyond the discomfort zone and into the *pain zone* on the other side. The further out you go, the more out of your depth you feel. There are less familiar landmarks. The world you see often seems a lot different to the world you're used to. There is often an incredibly steep learning curve. We often experience a series of setbacks (Heath, 2009). We encounter hurdles that we've never crossed before and questions we have never been asked before. Inevitably it requires a lot more work. We sometimes take emotional hits along the way if we don't get the results we were looking for after all of our efforts. We could start to question ourselves and ask whether we're actually capable of taking on the challenge we've set ourselves. It may take a long time to see results. As we noted in Chapter 4, our confidence will be more fragile if it is based on results. Therefore, to be happy stepping into our discomfort zone we need to ensure that we evaluate our processes, rather than judge our results (Gallwey, 1986; Dayton, 2007).

We've all had experiences like this. I remember back to those very early days of parenthood when we really didn't know what we were doing at times. Everything was new and unfamiliar. There were so many questions that we didn't have the answers to and situations we'd never encountered before. I also remember setting up businesses and working in new sectors and industries. The experience was very similar in many ways. There were an awful lot of setbacks and I tripped over a lot of hurdles.

The greatest hurdle for many people is often the risk of failure. This risk may even be a barrier that keeps them locked in their comfort zone. The perception of failure often causes people who enter their discomfort zone to endure it rather than embrace it and love it (Heath, 2009). The title of this chapter is 'Love your discomfort zone'. It is important to love it not just to endure it. If we love something, we're much more likely to seek it out. If we endure something, we're likely to only do it if we feel we have to. More often than not, we'll avoid doing it if possible. One of the best illustrations is physical exercise. Some people actively enjoy pushing their bodies. They like the feeling that their muscles are working and that they are out of breath. They like to know that they are testing themselves and pushing their capability. Personally, I like to know that I can do more today than I did last week. However, there are people who couldn't imagine anything worse. They can't understand why people would want to be out of breath, hot, sweaty and aching. Consequently, they will avoid exercise where possible, and do as little as possible when they absolutely have to exercise.

Fundamentally, we need to be happy making mistakes if we are to love our discomfort zone. We have to accept and embrace the fact that we will not get it right first time. In fact, we have to know that there may be some catastrophic failures along the way. Making mistakes, as we all know, is an essential part of learning. Sometimes our greatest errors can be our most powerful lessons (Halden-Brown, 2003; Heath, 2009). If we are scared of making mistakes, and scared of failing, we will probably stay firmly trapped inside our comfort zone. After all, when we're doing the things we're confident in and familiar with, we stand much more chance of getting them 'right'. When we get things 'right' we get that nice warm fuzzy feeling inside. When we get things 'wrong' our ego takes a knock, which tends not to feel nice. There is also a chance that other people will notice. If that's the case we also stand a chance of looking daft.

Here is a short piece from an article that I wrote for *Squash Player* magazine, entitled 'Learn From Everything':

"I've missed more than 9000 shots in my career. I've lost almost 300 games. 26 times, I've been trusted to take the game winning shot and missed. I've failed over and over and over again in my life. And that is why I succeed." Michael Jordan.

Michael Jordan is not alone. Most of the great people who have ever lived, have failed. Many of the great entrepreneurs went bust numerous times before they made serious money. The great artists and composers have torn up more work than they ever publish. Great athletes always miss more than they score and make more duff shots than perfect shots. And, as Michael Jordan says, that is the reason they succeed.

It's funny how most people hate making mistakes. As human beings, we tend to view mistakes as negative. We tend to view bad performances as negative and view losing as negative. In reality though, it's not the case. I agree that it's usually uncomfortable at the time because we want things to work perfectly all the time. We want things to come off perfectly first time and often get frustrated if the results don't show quickly enough.

Everyone knows that making mistakes is an important part of the learning process. However, there are relatively few people that embrace mistakes and celebrate them, or even who see them as a positive. Common advice is to forget about bad performances and put them behind you. However, the impact of losing or performing badly does often drive people to work harder on their game. Daft as it sounds, most people learn the least about their performance from victories or successes.

One of the characteristics of a truly great athlete is that they learn from everything – the good, the bad and the average. They learn from wonderful performances and dire performances equally. Those truly great athletes realize that to stay ahead they don't just need to move forwards. They actually need to move forwards quicker than everyone else, or they'll get overtaken. At the very pinnacle of every sport are athletes who have to constantly improve their game. They have to get better after every single training session and every single match they play. If they don't, they know that someone will overtake them.

(Hartley, 2010e: 24)

Human beings make mistakes. Sport psychologist and equestrian coach Susan Halden-Brown (2003) suggests that mistakes are not only inevitable, but also incredibly useful in sport. This sentiment is echoed by Tal Ben-Shahar (2009), who would advise us to forget about trying to eliminate mistakes and forget about trying to be perfect in life. Not only is it futile, it also stops us from growing, being happy and living our lives to the full.

Imagine if we scrapped the concept of 'right' and 'wrong' for a moment. I don't mean that we ditch our values and start murdering everyone. I simply mean that we drop the labels and the judgement we apply. If we could stop judging our efforts as 'right' or 'wrong', or as 'good' or 'bad', we could start to see them for what they actually are. Let's also imagine for a moment that it really didn't matter what other people thought. What if we weren't that interested in whether we looked good? What if we didn't care if we looked a bit daft? What if we didn't care whether people talked about us behind our backs or not? Imagine if you felt free to try something, knowing that if it didn't work perfectly it didn't matter. What if you just could try something knowing that mistakes were fine? In *The Art of Possibility*, Zander and Zander (2000) write about an orchestra rehearsal. During the rehearsal, someone made a mistake. Benjamin Zander, the conductor, stopped and said 'How fascinating!'. There was no judgement or negative reaction because the mistake was not 'wrong'. Let's take a step further and imagine that mistakes were actually celebrated because they were an essential part of learning, developing and growing? What if we saw mistakes and failure the same way as Michael Jordon does?

As human beings we have an infinite power to choose how we experience the world. Therefore, we have the choice to decide how we define success and failure (Manz, 2000, 2002). We can choose whether our discomfort zone is a threatening place because within it there is the prospect that we could fail. Our perception of mistakes and failure dictates how we feel. The meanings that we apply to the words 'mistakes' and 'failure' will underpin how we view them. We could embrace mistakes, knowing that they are actually constructive. We could redefine our view of failure.

Some people would not perceive that they'd failed simply because they attempted something that didn't work. Instead, they would see failure as not having attempted in the first place.

During the last few years I have been incredibly privileged to watch my children learn to walk. Just watching them has taught me a huge amount about learning and achievement. The first thing that I noticed was that they both fell down a lot. In fact, in the early stages they fell down constantly. In conventional terms, their success-to-failure ratio registered a 100 per cent failure rate. This didn't just continue for a day or two. It continued for several weeks, with many attempts every day. If we adults had tried multiple attempts per day for several weeks with a 100 per cent failure rate, we would probably have given up. Of course, infants don't give up, they keep trying. The difference is, they have no concept of failure. To them, falling over isn't 'wrong'. It's not a 'mistake'. So, they kept on trying. They didn't try the same way each time, they changed slightly and adapted. Gradually they started to change the success-to-failure ratio. They would balance just for a moment, then take a step, then two. They started to use supports less and walk independently more of the time. I'm sure you know the rest of the story.

The critical difference between children learning to walk and most of us attempting something new is the perception of failure. Infants don't have any concept of failure, so they keep going. Many adults try a handful of times and give up if it's not perfect. How many times have you heard, or uttered, the words 'I can't do it'. Normally, those words are the *reason* for our 'failure' not the *result* of it. If we changed our perception and said 'I can't do it perfectly yet', we may try some new ways and eventually succeed.

Criticism is often uncomfortable for us. When I was a student, I remember being disheartened when I took a piece of work to my tutor and found it returned with comments and suggestions (normally written in red ink). I wanted it to come back with just one word on it: 'perfect'. However, that never happened. After a while, my perception started to change. I actually started using the comments to improve my work and started to think differently about how I approached it. I would try to pre-empt the comments and make changes before I submitted the work. As I progressed through my studies, I became increasingly frustrated when there were less and less comments. I started to want the suggestions and looked forward to seeing the red ink. The criticism was actually helping me to get better. I can remember confronting my tutor one day and asking why there was no red ink on my work. Surely the work couldn't be perfect: there had to be something I could do to improve it. I'd started to thrive on the critical comments and knew that they were fuelling my growth.

In reality, it is often our ego that prevents us from loving our discomfort zone (Metzinger, 2010). My ego was stung by my tutor's criticism initially. It is our ego that worries about failing or looking silly. The ego worries about what people might think, or how we might be judged. The ego projects the image of what might happen if we get it wrong. And it is our ego that feels the pain if we judge that we have failed at something. I know this from personal experience because I've been there. I've tried things in my businesses that haven't worked out as planned. I've shed tears. I can remember sobbing on the phone to my Mum when we made the decision to move out of our dream house and downsize. The business venture that I'd been working on had not yielded the financial rewards that I needed. I felt like I'd failed. I had attempted something that had not produced the results I needed. We were desperately short of cash and we had no option other than to move out of the house we loved and into a smaller rental property. That hurt. My ego took a severe hit. My pride was definitely dented. In fact, if my pride had been a car, it would probably have been a write-off.

Transcending our ego is a very important step if we are to love our discomfort zone. Once we have moved beyond our ego and the fear of making mistakes or failing, we are free to become creative (Robinson, 2010). Creativity is enabled in our discomfort zone. Creativity, by definition, requires us to do something new. It requires innovation. We cannot be truly creative without stepping into the unknown. Creativity requires us to risk failing (Brown, 2008). I recently helped an organization to develop an environment that nurtures creativity. The principles are very simple. Firstly, the environment is free of judgement and allows people to experiment. There is no perfect model and therefore no right way or wrong way to do something. Because there is no right way or wrong way, we are open to new possibilities. We realize that there is a very real chance that somebody could come up with an entirely new solution that nobody has ever considered before. The new solution could be far more effective than anything we've seen so far and revolutionize current practice. Human beings are unique. The way we look at the world is unique. Therefore, by allowing everyone the freedom to experiment, we give ourselves the best chance of finding new solutions.

Here is a very practical illustration from *Street Soccer Coaching*, which is a handbook on creative coaching:

> The most effective way of producing a skill for one person will be different for another. Even the way each player kicks a ball will be individual. Every player's body is different, they have different sized feet, their limbs are different lengths, their weight is distributed differently, their centre of gravity is located in a different place in their body, their muscles are different sizes and all have different strength. So, how does it make sense to ask every player to conform to a textbook model?

Added to this, every player has a unique neurological system. The neural networks in our brain and our nervous system are created from the moment we start moving (even before we are born). As we move we start to build up networks by linking neurons so that we can produce movement patterns. We can see vast differences in the way that babies move. Babies may have only been moving and creating networks for a year or so. Imagine how different the neurological systems of 2 eight years olds will be. So, why would it make sense to make 2 very different eight year olds kick a ball the same way?

(Hartley and Laver, 2011: 7)

Many multi-billion pound businesses such as Google use this principle at the core of their creative process (Brown, 2008; Robinson, 2010). They know that when their people are free to play with ideas, they become creative. The link between play and creativity has been extensively researched within education (Lieberman, 1977). When we are free to play and express ourselves, we become creative (Brown, 2008). Tim Brown (2008), who cites the work of creativity researcher Bob McKim, also notes that when we fear that we will be judged we can become less likely to offer our ideas. We run the risk of embarrassing ourselves in front of our peers. However, when we are engaged in an activity for the simple pleasure of doing it, we will often experiment, try things differently and explore. We use our imagination to help us find new possibilities. This process leads us to find creative solutions. When we have a trusted environment where there is no judgement or fear of failure, we tend to be more willing to give things a go and see what happens. The more boundaries we have, the less experimentation we tend to do. If you've ever watched young children opening gifts at Christmas, you'll have noticed how much more interesting the box is to them than the gift inside it. Although it seems ironic to adults, to a child the box is far more interesting. Normally the toy does a few interesting things, but it has a fairly small number of possibilities. The box on the other hand has a vast number of possibilities. A box could be a house, a boat, a cave, a hide-out, a store, a plane or just about anything. When you're inside the box your world is a little different. With the box on top of you the world sounds different, looks different and probably smells different. The box becomes fascinating because it has endless possibilities. It engages our natural curiosity and our imagination starts to give it different meanings (Robinson, 2006, 2010). When these phenomena coincide, our natural creative juices flow. As we play, we try more things. As we try more things, we develop more neural connections. More networks, connections and links in our brain equals more intelligence (Caine and Caine, 1990). With more neural connections and more intelligence, we and our brains are able to adapt to novel situations more effectively. None of that happens in our comfort zone.

What happens if you don't operate in an environment that lends itself to creativity? What if your environment is judgemental and rigid? What if there is a very clear definition of 'right', 'wrong', 'good' and 'bad' and you're expected to simply get things 'right'? What if your management environment demands that you get it right every time without fail?

You manage your internal environment (Glasser, 1999). You choose how your internal environment is governed. You have the power to decide whether you push yourself into your discomfort zone or not. You decide whether you let your ego, or the risks of failure, constrict you. Moving into your discomfort zone doesn't mean that you have to revolutionize the world. You don't need to invent the next microchip. It could simply be that you challenge yourself to find better, more efficient or more effective ways to do things. You could challenge yourself to do things at a higher standard, more precisely or more consistently. You could work to improve your skills, techniques, approaches or strategies. Rather than shying away from critical comments, you could seek them out and use them to help you improve. These are all examples of moving beyond your comfort zone. You are the only one who can dictate whether you operate in your comfort zone or your discomfort zone. The simple fact is that if we want to achieve peak performance, we need to operate at the edge of our capabilities (Csikszentmihalyi, 1990). Alistair White's (2009) model, from performance management, shows that the *Optimal Performance Zone* lies outside of the comfort zone.

In conclusion, it seems that to achieve peak performance we need to be challenged and we need to venture into our discomfort zone.

Summary

- Our discomfort zone is where we learn, grow and improve.
- To love our discomfort zone, we need to embrace and use our mistakes positively.
- To embrace and use our mistakes, we may need to change the way we perceive them.
- To embrace our mistakes, we may need our ego to take a back seat so that we can risk 'failing'.
- Challenge yourself, push yourself and explore new territory.
- Giving up is the reason we fail, not the result of failure.

8

Release the hand brake!

A few years ago I was working with a long jumper. We were discussing his performance. He was becoming frustrated because he felt that he wasn't jumping freely. He recalled that when he was a little younger he would charge down the runway for all he was worth and just launch himself into the air. He didn't really have any technique to speak of at the time. In fact, he'd probably have been referred to as a 'raw talent'. However, that seemed to have changed now. He had been working on his technique and was a far more accomplished jumper now, in many ways. He was also stronger, faster and more powerful. But, the athlete felt as if there was something missing. He felt as if he was not quite at full throttle. In the course of our conversation I asked him 'do you feel like you're performing with the hand brake on?'.

As I looked at other athletes, I saw the same signs. Performers looked like they were performing in some sort of a mental straight jacket. At the time, I wondered if this was specific to athletes. In the case of our long jumper, this might simply have been a symptom of over-thinking and the fact that he was concentrating too heavily on his technique (Flegal and Anderson, 2008). Was his mind too full of thoughts to just run and jump? As we talked about it over the course of a few sessions, I started to conclude that *the mental hand brake* is actually something that pervades throughout life. It's not restricted to sport.

Most of us probably live life with our hand brake on to a certain extent. We normally hold something back. We keep something in reserve. At times we find ourselves playing our cards too close to our chest rather than wearing our hearts on our sleeves. It's as if we're scared to show the world all of who we are and what we've got. In short, we don't give fully of ourselves. In the UK we would probably see this trait as 'very British'. Is it culturally ingrained? Does it come from the 'stiff upper lip' school of emotional awareness?

I have to admit, I still haven't got to the bottom of this myself. I find myself living my life with the hand brake on at times. I often ask myself what it is that keeps me from putting the hand brake to the floor and pushing the throttle as far as it will go. Perhaps it is the fear that I will give it everything that I've got and not succeed? I met a swimmer once who told me that she would never give everything she had. She told me that if she kept something in reserve, she could console herself afterwards with the idea that she might have been able to win if she had given it her all. It was a mental safety net. Her alternative was to know that she'd given it everything she had and it wasn't good enough. In that situation, she would have no hiding place. She'd have no excuse. She would have to admit that her best wasn't good enough to win (Reitman and Williams, 1961).

Perhaps we use mental hand brakes if we have a fear of success? Fear of success can be just as paralysing as fear of failure (Miller, 1994). Many people may fear success because it tests their limits and makes them vulnerable to new situations. New challenges are presented, which take us into our discomfort zone. Often success will take us into uncharted territory and break our status quo. Imagine the changes that come when you take a business from sole trader status and start employing people. What happens when you go from a handful of employees to 50, or 100, or more? Imagine all of the new demands. The world will start to change very quickly. You'd have administration, finance, HR and management concerns. You'd be taken out of being a practitioner and become a manager. Although you've always said that you want to run a big business, when it comes to the crunch do you truly want the things that would go with it? Success could mean a big change (Midgley and Abrams, 1974).

Even worse, success can expose weaknesses and force people to deal with their flaws. Success is scary when it involves change. Success can be intimidating and hard to handle. With success come more challenge and more responsibilities, which can be threatening. Sometimes people fear success because they don't know if they can live up to their achievements. They don't think they're good enough or smart enough. They're afraid they don't have what it takes to rise to the challenge, and they don't know if they can sustain their success. Psychologist Roy Baumeister and colleagues observed that success can often lead to increased pressure on a performance, and not just increased confidence (Baumeister, Hamilton and Tice, 1985). This often happens when success is public, and performers perceive that there is therefore an increase in expectation. I have seen this a lot in athletes. The athletes believe that if they give a spectacular performance, everyone will expect them to repeat it (Anderson, 2000). The problem is, the athlete doesn't know whether they can. Part of them might think it is a fluke. Stuart Dunkel (1989) notes that the same phenomenon is often seen in musicians during the audition process.

Maybe a part of it stems from fear of rejection (Verbeke and Bagozzi, 2000). I can remember my hand brake being firmly on when I was at school. I wasn't enamored with the prospect of approaching girls and asking them out. What if they said 'no'? My poor little ego couldn't quite handle the idea. I probably felt that if this girl said 'no', all the others would probably say 'no' as well. If she doesn't want to go out with me, why would any of the others? I see the same trait in sales people often, especially when things aren't going well. Rejections seem to carry the same meaning as they did for me at school. If this person won't buy, why would the next person (Verbeke et al., 2000)? When we take on this mindset, we often change our behaviour. We start avoiding situations. We are torn between wanting to do something, but avoiding it because it might lead to rejection. We've probably made a link between rejection and failure (Seaward, 2006). Rejection can hurt (Seaward, 2006). If we think that rejection means that we are not good enough, we're unlikely to put ourselves in a situation where we would experience that – and on comes our hand brake.

Perhaps, though, there is another reason. Maybe we are nervous about pushing ourselves to our limit because it takes us to *the edge* (Clash, 2003). How often have we ever been absolutely at the limits of our capability? For most of us, it's unknown territory. We simply don't know what *the edge* is. We don't know what it feels like to be there. It would almost be like stepping onto another planet. What if we couldn't breathe? What if it was too hot? What if our body and mind simply couldn't cope and we blacked out? What if it was just too scary?

There is a distinct possibility that many of us keep the hand brake on because we're scared of losing control (Midgley and Abrams, 1974). When I talk to athletes about releasing the hand brake, we often use the words 'letting go'. Our hand brake gives us control. It stops us from speeding out of control and allows us to do things at a comfortable pace and on our terms. Letting go often means that we must relinquish control. In order to do that we need to trust. The element of ourself that has control is our conscious brain, which normally operates under the direction of our ego (Baumeister, Heatherton and Tice, 1993;

Moller, Deci and Ryan, 2006). To start releasing our hand brake we need to be confident enough to switch off our conscious brain and allow our unconscious to take over (Gallwey, 1986). Those people who are control freaks often have the hand brake firmly on.

Let's have a look at the case of our long jumper. We spent a few weeks working on an exercise to help him release his mental hand brake. He found that he was starting to put the brakes on, literally, because he wasn't confident he could control his speed on the runway. During the winter he'd become faster and more powerful. Running at full pace seemed quite scary to him, because it was unfamiliar. It probably felt a little bit like riding down a steep hill on a bike with dodgy brakes. Added to this, he wasn't sure how to control this speed on the take-off board, and feared that his technique would be compromised. The result was that he slowed down as he approached the board, rather than accelerating.

We started by making the athlete aware of his hand brake. After a while he could quite accurately tell whether he was running at 70 per cent, 80 per cent or 100 per cent. In fact, he became accurate to within 2 or 3 per cent. His next challenge was to deliberately control his hand brake. We started experimenting with different speeds of run-up. He would try some at 70, some at 85, some at 95, one at 80, one at 100 per cent. Although his aim was to control the jump as well as possible, there was no success or failure. We were not particularly worried about the outcome of the jump. The point of the exercise was to control the hand brake and become familiar and more comfortable with the hand brake released. Over the course of several weeks, he started to make 85–90 per cent jumps consistently in control. This then progressed until he was happy attempting near 100 per cent jumps, and eventually controlling them.

Motor racing drivers have a similar mental demand to other elite athletes (Hardcastle, 2008). They need to operate on a knife edge (Clash, 2003). They need to push themselves and the car to the absolute limit of their capability. But it is a fine line. If they over-step the mark they risk crashing. The consequences of crashing in motor sport could potentially be fatal. However, if they don't push themselves and the car to the limit, they will probably be beaten. If their performance drops by just 1 per cent, it might make the difference between winning and not even scoring a point. For most of us, the prospect would be daunting enough in dry conditions with no other cars on the circuit. Obviously the challenge increases in a competitive situation with wet tyres and spray everywhere.

Do you know where the edge is? Do you know what you are truly capable of? Do you know where your ceiling is? Can you say you have been to the very limit of your capability and given it absolutely everything you had? If so, how did it feel?

The exercise with our long jumper is incredibly simple and can be applied to any walk of life by employing the same process. Firstly, you need to be aware of your hand brake. You need to know when the hand brake is on fully and when you've released it slightly. You need to be able to grade it between *fully on* and *fully released*. Once you're aware of this, you can start to deliberately take control and start experimenting. Releasing your hand brake will require challenging yourself on the things that are currently holding you back. You'll need to step into your discomfort zone and start taking on the things that are causing you to pull the hand brake on. You'll need to let go and relinquish control of the things you've been holding onto. You'll have to let go of the things that you've been holding onto for protection. For example, you could:

- do the things that you'd really love to do but don't feel you have the nerve to do;

- dance and don't care what anyone else thinks. So what if they think you look daft? So what if it's not in rhythm?
- sing your heart out and don't care whether it's in tune or not;
- run naked on the beach with the wind in your hair.

I have a few friends who genuinely live life with their hand brake off. They don't tend to show any signs of inhibitions. They don't seem to worry what anyone else will think of them. People who live life with the hand brake off seem to have a far greater sense of freedom. I recently went on a business trip for a week with one particular friend who exemplifies this. I've known this friend most of my adult life, so I'd say I know him pretty well. However, it still surprises me just how enigmatic he can be. Our trip took us to a country that neither of us had been to before. We didn't know anyone, other than our liaison, and we didn't speak a word of the language. Those are not barriers to my friend, they are minor technicalities. They certainly didn't stop my mate engaging everyone he met.

The purpose of our trip was to research the standard of the nation's football and their readiness to qualify for the World Cup. In order to do this we needed to understand their current standard of football across the board, from the kids in the street to the current national team. We turned up one evening at a playground in the middle of the capital. My friend set up some speed testing equipment and got some of the kids who were playing football to come over and do some sprint tests. My mate is a big character, full of energy and he always wears a smile. The kids of course took to him immediately. 'Who is the fastest?' he said to them (in English). Within 5 minutes he'd got kids coming from everywhere to have a go and test themselves. After 20–30 minutes we'd found some winners, given out some baseball caps and had a great set of data.

How many people would just have wandered into a playground full of teenagers in an Arab capital city and started running sprint tests? Most people's fears or uncertainty would probably have started to conjure up all sorts of reasons why they couldn't just get stuck in. They would need an interpreter. They'd need it to be pre-arranged and organized. My friend didn't need an interpreter. He had a smile. He had that easy self-assured confidence and the natural energy that comes with genuine enthusiasm. That's all he needed. In fact, in most situations, those ingredients tend to work just fine.

So, what is it that gives people this freedom? How can they operate without all the reserves and safeguards that most people use? What is it that allows them to just dive in without the concerns or fears that might cause the rest of us to stutter? Here's one answer:

> They *know* themselves . . . and they are *happy* with themselves. . . therefore, they can *be* themselves!

Is this an ancient wisdom that most of us have forgotten? (Aristotle, trans. 1976; Corlett, 1996). Herein lies perhaps the greatest single secret to success in my humble opinion. How many people genuinely know themselves? One of the hardest questions in life is 'who are you?'. I often ask people that question. Initially, most will answer by telling me their roles, or their labels. They might tell me their name, which is a label. They might tell me their job, or their role within a family. For example, my name is Simon Hartley, I am a husband, a father and a performance coach.

None of those responses tells me who Simon Hartley is. The person that we are endures and is not dependent on any life circumstances, such as jobs or family situations. I would not become a different person if I changed my name or stopped being a performance coach. I was not a different person the day before I married or the day before my first daughter was born. I'll admit that there are aspects of me that have changed as a result of those events, but the core of who I am remains.

Some people will try to go one stage further and add some form of evaluation or judgement to their labels. For example, they might say 'I'm a pretty good husband', 'a very experienced performance coach' or a 'successful businessman'. However, those are just extensions of our roles and labels. They still don't answer the question 'who are you?' (Potter, 2010).

In order to get the real answers, we need to look more deeply at ourselves. We can start by becoming self-aware (Bach, 1974), and reflecting on ourselves in our lives. We need to look at how we tend to react in various situations, how we think, how we feel in different circumstances, what affects us and what doesn't. Here are some questions that I've used to start the thought process:

- When are you kind and helpful? When do you tend not to be? What dictates how kind and helpful you might be?
- When are you generous? When do you tend not to be? What dictates how generous you might be?
- When are you a good friend? Do you make and break friendships quickly? What would cause you to break off a friendship?
- When are you hard working? When do you push yourself hardest? What motivates you and what turns you off completely?
- When are you focused? When do you get distracted more easily?
- When do you enjoy life the most? When don't you enjoy life?
- When are you optimistic and when are you pessimistic?
- How do you respond to difficult challenges? How do you respond to knocks? How many times would you

take a knock before you gave up? When do knocks hurt you?

- How do you respond to criticism? How do you respond to praise? How do you respond to rejection?
- When do you find that you let other people get to you, and when do you tend not to be bothered? What would they have to say? Have you got an Achilles heel? If so, what is it?
- How do you think of other people? How judgemental are you? What do you tend to be judgemental about? What do you tend to criticize other people for? What do you praise other people for?
- In what situations would you feel safe and secure, threatened and afraid, happy, sad, confident, nervous, serious, silly, angry, calm, frustrated, patient, determined, strong and powerful or weak and helpless? Who or what could change your thoughts and emotions? Who could do it and what would they have to do or say?

The answers to these sorts of questions start to build up a picture of who we are. I know, for example, that I tend to make and break relationships fairly easily. I do have a number of friendships that I've had for many years. Those tend to be enduring but I have been known to completely cut people out of my life if they have breached one of my core values. On several occasions, I have severed a friendship because I suspected that the person had been dishonest (lied or stolen) or betrayed another friend of mine. I tend not to be very forgiving under those circumstances. I also tend to be generous but I normally exercise this with people close to me and my generosity tends to reflect how affluent I am feeling at the time. In most situations I will give my best, but I remember occasions when I didn't like or respect the person I was working for. I didn't feel that they deserved my best, so I did just enough to get by.

We are complex individuals. Very rarely do we follow black and white rules. We don't tend to always react one way or another. In order to understand ourselves, we need to know how we think, feel, behave and respond. This will tell us an awful lot about our values and beliefs. For example, how we judge others will tell us a lot about how we judge ourselves and about what we believe is important. For example, do we judge other people by their body fat percentage? If so, we're probably not going to be too proud about our own flabby bits and we'll work hard to cover them up. If we judge being fat as 'bad', we'll have a negative view of ourself if we feel that we're overweight. We're unlikely to be comfortable in the nude. We won't want to show the world who we are, in all our glory, because there are bits of us we're ashamed of (Potter, 2010).

Do we make judgements about people based on their finances? Do we judge people by the car they drive, the clothes they wear or the house they live in? If so, we're likely to judge ourselves in the same way. We're likely to be ashamed if we drive a 10-year-old car that's looking the worse for wear. Would we proudly drive up to the entrance in it or sheepishly park it around the corner and walk? How will we feel about ourselves when we're driving it? If we feel that making money is a product of being successful, will we judge that this car is a sign that we're failing?

Deeper self-knowledge requires us to answer some of the more fundamental questions. Self-knowledge focuses on knowing who we are, our values, what we stand for and our deepest beliefs (Valle and Halling, 1989; Nesti, 2004).

If we believe that we're not what we want to be, we won't be happy being ourselves. Why would you be yourself if you weren't happy with who you were? By being yourself, you'd allow the world to see who you are. If you aren't happy with yourself you won't be yourself. Instead, your ego will try to create an image of the person you want to be, and project that to the world (Epstein, 2006; Metzinger, 2010). If you're not happy being yourself, your ego will start trying to portray a different you. You'll try to convince the world that you are actually the person you wish you were. Your ego will try to hide your 'faults'. It will try to create a mask and a facade. It will put on a brave face when things are going badly. You will be diplomatic to someone when you are face to face with them, whilst your mind is being judgemental. Your ego will criticize other people openly, to demonstrate how different from them you are. Your ego will pull others down to make yourself appear greater. Ultimately, if we don't believe that our 'self' is good enough, we won't be happy with it and we won't present it to the world (Chopra, Williamson and Ford, 2010).

When we find ourselves in that pattern, we are living life with the hand brake on! We're reserved and guarded. We are trying to be someone we're not, which takes a great deal of effort. It is not free and effortless. It is defensive. We end up being governed by what we imagine others will think of us. Our mind is so tied up being concerned with our image, it's not free to just *be* (Bach, 1974; Vajda, 2008).

I think it all comes back to how we define success (Frankl, 1959/1984). Our ego tries desperately to make us appear successful in whatever we believe is important. If we're in business, our ego wants the world to see that we're a great business person. If we're an athlete, the ego wants to show the world what a great athlete we are. The criteria for success are therefore set out for us. If it's business, the criteria might be money. In sport, it could be a ranking, medal haul, number of caps for your country, Grand Slam wins, records or championship titles.

What if we changed our definition of success? What if success meant being ourself and being true to ourself? Socrates would probably argue that being yourself is *the* number one goal in life (Aristotle, trans. 1976). Everything else is secondary. If we made loads of money but were not ourself, in Socrates eyes that would constitute failure. If we won 50 Olympic gold medals and we failed to be ourself, it could also be argued that we'd missed the point. In fact, it could also be argued that we'd worked so hard to make the money or win the medals that we wouldn't need to be ourself. Instead of being ourself, we could then hide behind the money or the medals and try to convince ourself we had been successful. Whatever other failings we may have, we could console ourself by focusing on the money or the medals and pretend that all was well.

What if we swapped our priorities? What if we decided that being ourself *was* success? What if our aim in any given task or situation was to understand ourself and be ourself (May, 1953)? Life has a way of challenging us in everything we do. Situations will tempt you away from being yourself in some way. We might be tempted away by the prospect of money, reward, fame or recognition. Equally, we might be tempted by the thought of being exposed, embarrassed, ridiculed or humiliated (Vajda, 2008). Whatever the situation, Socrates would probably say that our job was simply to be authentic and true to ourself. These are profound concepts that have been at the centre of philosophy for centuries (Hatzimoysis, 2010). I would argue that they are also central to our lives every day (May, 1953).

I remember having a conversation with a very good friend of mine who was my PhD tutor and my BASES (British Association of Sport and Exercise Sciences) Accreditation supervisor. It was whilst I was working in Premiership football. I was in a culture that didn't match any of my values. Players didn't want to be the best that they could be. It was not a culture of excellence; it was a culture of excuses. Rather than working hard to turn around their performance, the players backed away. At the helm was a manager who was rude and disrespectful. I felt completely out of place. I felt like an ice cube in boiling water. At one point it struck me that I had two choices, either change myself to become part of the culture, or leave. It was a highly paid job at the pinnacle of my profession. I'd worked all of my professional life to get to that point. The choice was easy. I left.

A few years later I found myself having a similar conversation with that very same friend. I was working as an executive director in a fast-start business, under a chief executive officer whose vision, values and messages were changing. We started the business with an agreed set of values. Those values had started disintegrating. At one point I remarked that the goal posts had moved so far that I wasn't quite sure I was on the same pitch any more, or even playing the same sport. I could see parallels developing with my experience in the football club and said to my friend 'if it's a choice between changing my job or changing myself, I'll be changing the job'. A little while later, I left.

I believe that being yourself is central to living life with the hand brake off. Once we can start to live and perform with the hand break off, we give ourselves a fighting chance of performing at our peak. If we leave the hand brake on, we stand very little chance. Many people assume that the best way to go faster is to push the throttle. Let's be honest, we can push the throttle all we like, but if we've got the brakes on we're not going to get far. With brakes on and throttle to the floor, we'll just create friction and eventually burn out the engine. If we let the brakes off first, we could even switch off the engine and freewheel downhill with effortless speed.

Summary

- Often our ego causes us to live our life with the hand brake on.
- Know yourself. Understand who you are, not the labels that describe what you do.
- Be happy with yourself.
- Be yourself.
- Does it really matter what everyone else thinks?
- Review your definition of success. Perhaps being successful *is* being yourself.

9

Avoid the trapdoors

Life is simple but we insist on making it
complicated.

(Confucius, a long time ago)

Sport, business and life are actually pretty simple when we
strip them back to the basics. If we took everything on its
own merit, our lives would be a doddle. However, as human
beings we have a tendency to confuse everything. We add a
lot of garbage into the mix and we often lose sight of the
simple task in front of us. We take a molehill and turn it
into a mountain. How difficult is it really to sink a 3 foot
putt? If you're not a golfer, it might be a challenge. If you've
practised putting for years, it's a pretty easy task (Fisher,
1998). How difficult is it to deliver a sales pitch? If you're
not a sales executive, it might be a challenge. If you've been
selling all your life, it's pretty easy.

How is it possible then that a golfer could feel nervous
standing over a 3 foot putt? What if we put a gun to their
head and told them that we'd shoot them if they missed?
Would that change the task? Would the challenge all of
a sudden change from sinking a putt to saving a life?
What if we had a big red button instead? If the golfer
misses the putt we will press the big red button and
detonate the Earth. Does the challenge now change from
sinking a putt to saving the World or is it still a 3 foot putt
(Fisher, 1998)?

If the golfer thinks that the challenge is to save the Earth, he'll probably see that as a tough one. He may not have saved the World before, so there is a chance that he'll see it as impossible. All of a sudden the 3 foot putt starts to take on a new meaning. We've complicated the very simple task and turned it into a monster. Our little molehill just became a mountain. All too often we do exactly the same things in our lives. The example of the golfer saving the World is perhaps a little extreme, but we have a habit of applying the same process to many simple tasks. When we do this, we start to create trapdoors for ourselves. These trapdoors are scattered in our path as we try to navigate through our lives. Most people are unaware of them, until they step on one and start to experience the sensation of falling. Before they know what's happened, they are struggling to perform things that should be simple for them. They're so caught up in the negative spiral – the pressure and the anxiety – that they almost forget how to perform. In gymnastics there is a condition that is known as 'lost move syndrome' (Day, Thatcher, Greenlees and Woods, 2006). It refers to a phenomenon where the gymnast will simply not be able to execute a move that they have done hundreds of times before.

A few years ago I worked with a gymnast. He was a Great Britain International and specialized in the trampoline. He had developed 'lost move syndrome' for one move in particular, but noticed that it was starting to affect other moves as well. When we started talking, it became apparent that it was a symptom of over-thinking. As he took off, his mind started asking 'what if . . .?'. Initially it was 'what if I don't land on the cross?' and over time this evolved into 'what if I don't land properly and I hurt myself?' As you can imagine, things happen very quickly when the gymnast is in the air. There really isn't time for a conversation in your mind. The window to exit the somersault lasts for a split second and the gymnast has to time it just right. There is no way that the thinking brain can find that point because it flashes past too quickly. The sub-conscious, non-thinking brain finds it no problem. So, imagine how scary it would be to try to perform the skill with your thinking brain. Imagine how hard it would be to consciously get your timing exactly right. Even to an experienced gymnast, that is a near-impossible task. The only way to perform the skill (and find the perfect exit point) is to trust and allow the non-thinking brain to perform naturally as it has done hundreds of times before (Gallwey, 1986).

So what is it that caused our gymnast to start thinking? Let's have a look at the start of the 'what ifs'. It all started because the athlete was concerned that he might not hit the cross perfectly. The cross on the trampoline is there for good reason. It's right in the centre and therefore gives the gymnast the best take-off for the next move. If he'd missed the cross a few times and found the next few moves more difficult, it may have affected his routine. So, how does that suddenly become 'lost move syndrome', not just in one move but in a number of different moves?

The answer is that our gymnast fell down a trapdoor. Hitting the cross started to become an issue because it had an impact on the result. Our gymnast started to get caught up in the outcome and therefore started over-thinking. He started getting sucked into the negative spiral that we discussed in the Introduction (Lindsley et al., 1995). He made a mistake, started to analyze and over-think and therefore produced another mistake. Normally, the mistakes then start to become bigger and bigger. On the trampoline, when mistakes become too big you risk injury.

We all create our own trapdoors. Normally, they are created because we are tying ourselves to the results and the outcome in some way. We've started to over-complicate our simple task by adding an outcome to it. When we do that, we run the risk of perceiving that the outcome lies beyond our capability. We set ourselves an impossible task. In the case of our gymnast, we need to start dismantling the trapdoor. We need to understand why the outcome has so much importance to him. We need to allow him to see the task for what it is. His job is not to save the World, it is to execute a skill that he's done hundreds of times before. He doesn't have to do it perfectly. He has to execute it to the best of his ability. With practice, his best will be better next week than it is today and even better in a few weeks' time.

Our gymnast had actually fallen down a trapdoor that many people create for themselves. He'd started to link his success on the trampoline to success in life. Trampolining had taken on an artificial level of importance. All of a sudden, this move was not just a move any more. The routine was not just a linked series of moves that he could execute in his sleep. Instead, it constituted a huge proportion of his self-worth. His performance on the trampoline was being used as a measure of his success as a person. Success in sport had started to equal success in life. That is a very dangerous place to be. In that situation, we start to pin all of our self-worth to the performance. If we mess up the performance, we are nothing (Covington, 1984, 1992).

Here's an excerpt from a session with an elite junior rower:

> We talked for quite a while about your reasons for rowing. I'm always keen to really challenge an athlete's reasons for doing what they do – it's a kind of stress test. You mentioned your friends and also said that getting good scores and being successful are big reasons to row. Like many athletes, there is not much time left in your life (after rowing and school) for a lot else. So rowing plays a big part in your life. The potential danger with this is that if everything (your happiness in life, feeling successful, etc.) hinges on success in rowing, you create a great deal of pressure on yourself to

perform. You start to see that if rowing goes wrong, life goes wrong, because rowing is so important to you. This is a very fragile position to be in!

Does that mean that we shouldn't want success? Surely that can't be right. In Chapter 5 we said that motivation is underpinned by 'really wanting something'. However, it can be a double-edged sword, especially if *want* turns into *need*. Here's another piece from a summary report that I wrote for an elite junior football player:

> There is always an 'up' side and a 'down' side to *wanting it*. When you're on the field, you need to have the desire to win the ball, get to it first, stay strong in the challenge, etc. However, a lot of players start to worry about what will happen if they don't succeed. A lot of players have a fear of losing what they have or what they dream of having. If you've got fear, you're screwed. Watch *Star Wars III* if you get a chance and listen to Yoda talking to Anakin Skywalker about why fear of losing something is always going to screw you up. Yoda warns Anakin against looking into the future. He explains that fear of loss is the path to the dark side and that attachment has its dangers. Finally, Yoda says, 'train yourself to let go of everything you fear to lose'.
>
> To get around this, I think it's really important to have a great safety net. What if you weren't playing football? What would you do if you were injured and the Doc told you that you'd never play again? You have to be happy with a future where you weren't playing pro football. If you know you have a great future with or without football, you'll not have that fear of losing it.

Interestingly, philosophers Kevin Decker and Jason Eberl (2005) also use the film *Star Wars* to illustrate that lack of self-knowledge leads to loss of self-control and anxiety.

Working with an elite junior fencer recently has given me perhaps the most striking example (excuse the pun). The fencer trains and competes as part of an elite squad that is based regionally. He is one of the top two or three in the country in his age group and discipline. As with most elite athletes, he spends a lot of time fencing. His world is largely made up of fencing. His friends are fencers. His social life is fencing. Whenever he's not at school he is training or competing. As with many other athletes, life *is* fencing. The people that form his immediate society all live and breathe fencing too. Fencing is therefore incredibly important to them as well. As a result, fencing starts to take on a different and artificial meaning. It now becomes a means of creating a social standing. Rankings start to become the basis on which the social hierarchy is formed. It is almost like a monetary currency.

As you can imagine, all this baggage starts to form the trapdoor for the fencer. It becomes important to win so that he can maintain his social standing. He gets frustrated and angry if he starts losing points to lower ranked opponents. He loses sight of the task in front of him and starts focusing on the spectators. Fencing could be easy. It could simply be a case of trying to hit the opponent before the opponent hits you. On the other hand, it could be a mission to become an important, recognized person and gain the respect of a community. Clark Sorensen (1994) found the same patterns within education, in situations where academic achievement is closely linked with social class.

In our example, fencing is being used as a way of establishing and confirming self-worth. Poor performance equals low self-worth. Losing equals low self-worth. I think we've just found a trapdoor: 'A gold medal is a wonderful thing, but if you're not enough without it, you'll never be enough with it' (Irv Blitzer [John Candy], from the film *Cool Runnings*).

This situation is very true in business environments, medical environments, local politics and general life too. Martin Covington (1992) has studied the same phenomena in education. I've seen the same with sales teams. I've seen it within boardrooms and executive teams. When I was younger, I saw it in the local Scouting Association. I saw people's self-worth tied to their title. Grown adults were scrabbling to become the next 'assistant district commissioner' because it gave them some social standing.

This all becomes exacerbated if we start to hype up our performances. How often have you seen people talk themselves up, and then crumble under the 'pressure' to then deliver (Baumeister et al., 1985)? It happens with colleagues in businesses, with elite athletes and even with mates playing a round on the golf course. Our friend the ego is in the driving seat as usual and starts to create our trapdoors for us. There are fantastic illustrations in the media. TV shows such as *The Apprentice* are prime examples. Sports such as boxing and football are also characterised by ego-fuelled media hype, which can create trapdoors for performers.

In Chapter 8 we discussed the role that our ego plays. Our ego is concerned with our image and our identity (Lapsley and Power, 1988). To make the ego's life easier, it starts to apply all sorts of labels to help us identify ourself. A lot of athletes associate themselves very strongly with their labels. Academics often refer to 'athletic identity', because a lot of sportspeople identify themselves so closely with their sport (Sparkes, 1998). We often do this when the activity that we're identifying ourselves with is important to us. I once played cricket. I was absolute garbage. My highest score ever was three not out. I once bowled an over with eight wides. I never referred to myself as 'a cricketer', because being good at cricket never held any importance to me. It was something I did on a Sunday with my college mates and nothing more. However, when I was at college I did refer to myself as 'a rugby player'. I spent a lot of time training, playing and helping run the student team. Therefore, it made up a large part of my identity.

Although adopting an identity is something we naturally do, it can also cause us to create trapdoors. We usually start applying a judgement in addition to the identity. We'll start by saying 'I am a sales executive' (for example). However, that's not usually enough for our ego. Our ego would like to think of itself as *good*. So, we set ourselves a target of being a good sales executive. The problem is, when we're not selling very much, our ego could conclude that we're a bad sales executive. If being a sales executive is important to our identity, and being good is important to us, we're in a vulnerable position if it goes wrong. If we hadn't aligned ourselves strongly with that identity, we would probably not have worried too much if we were not selling. I wasn't particularly worried that I only scored three runs and never took a wicket on the cricket field because I didn't consider myself to be 'a cricketer'.

Perhaps the solution is to have a broad sense of identity. If your self-identity hinges on one thing, you will tend to place a great deal of pressure on that one thing (Symes, 2010). In this scenario, your identity is dependent on your success. If you have a wide range of things with which you identify, you'll be able to take a more measured view. But how does that work for an athlete who spends most of their waking life focused on their sport? How does it work for a businessman who spends 16–18 hours a day working on their business? What else can they focus on?

In Chapter 8 we discussed the importance of knowing yourself. As we said, our roles and labels change. They are situational. At the age of 65, the likelihood is that the 'athlete' will not be an athlete any more. At the age of 85, the business person may not be in business. Therefore, maybe we should identify ourselves with who we are, rather than our roles. Perhaps we should ensure that our sense of self-worth is governed by how we live our lives, not on our sales performance, the turnover of the business, our titles or our ranking (May, 1953). Some athletes face a major challenge when they come to the end of their competitive career (Grove, Lavallee and Gordon, 1997). Most athletes have held a strong connection with their athletic identity since they were small. All of a sudden, their identity is questioned. If they are not an athlete any more, who are they? It is often the same for other people as they retire. If they are not the chief executive officer of the company, who are they? People with a broad sense of self find that they answer those questions much more easily. Their *self* is not dependent upon one particular thing, and they don't need success in a specific field in order to find self-worth.

A little while ago, I worked with a middle-distance runner who was really struggling. He had been injured for a prolonged period and his physiotherapist was concerned that there were other issues starting to develop. The athlete was finding it hard being 'an athlete' who wasn't running. Running was his life and being an athlete was his identity. His athletics gave him a sense of self-pride. Now that he couldn't train or compete, that source of self-pride had dried up. As a result, the athlete had found himself caught in a downward spiral.

The lack of self-pride meant that he didn't really like himself very much. Because he didn't like himself very much, he didn't treat himself very well. He wasn't eating well so he felt tired and lethargic. His body was therefore slower to heal. The knock-on effect was that he became de-motivated and viewed himself as lazy. He couldn't work out why he was being lazy, because he valued hard work and achievement. As a person who placed importance on hard work, lazy was not something he enjoyed viewing himself as. Therefore, he didn't like himself very much and the spiral continued.

The athlete needed to break the cycle. The solution was simply to start liking himself again. The athlete could not use his training and competition performances any more. In fact, he could not use athletics or his identity as an athlete any more. Therefore, he had to start looking at himself in other ways. I asked him what he valued in people. He came up with around eight things, including 'hard working', 'kind, self-less and helpful', 'generous' and 'comfortable and happy with themselves'. I then asked him how his friends would describe him in those terms. How hard working would they say he was? How generous, how helpful and how self-less? We started to create a picture of how he felt he was viewed by those who knew him best, and also how he viewed himself. Typically, he viewed himself more modestly than he felt others would view him. Nevertheless, we started to broaden his sense of self. Of course, there were elements that he didn't think were perfect, so we set out to help him improve on those areas. Gradually he began to focus on his true self, rather than his narrow athletic identity. He also developed the areas of himself that he wished to improve. As a result, he was able to be happy with himself as a person, not just as an athlete (Nesti, 2004).

The process that our runner went through did not happen overnight. I genuinely believe that significant changes take time and effort. I often use the phrase 'real change requires real changes' when I'm working with people. For many people, the process can be quite uncomfortable (Nesti, 2004). We often need to take a real hard look at ourselves and start to ask some serious questions. We need to address things that we've previously put off, brushed under the carpet or chosen to overlook. I tend to refer to this process as 'turning out our boxes'.

Imagine an attic full of boxes. The boxes typically contain our memories. We have accumulated them throughout our lives. They normally have trinkets, photo albums or old letters and cards. When it comes to physical objects, we normally tend to keep the nice things or the things that we want to have around us and want to remember. Whenever I've moved house it always seems to take two or three times as long as it should because we end up finding all of the photo albums and scrapbooks, which we reminisce over.

The same thing happens in our minds. We accumulate memories and experiences and store them away. This is referred to as the Personal Unconscious within psychology (Jung, 1968). Some of these memories and experiences might be positive, others will be negative. However, we don't often choose whether we keep hold of them or throw them out. Normally, we keep them all, especially the ones that are associated with powerful emotions. For example, an experience that came with a deep feeling of guilt will tend to stay with us. As a result, we have a mental attic full of boxes. Some of those boxes contain things we don't really like or don't want to look at (Bach, 1974; Nesti, 2004). We try to fool ourselves into thinking that if we ignore them they will go away. Perhaps if we just keep doing what we do each day they'll magically resolve themselves. Hopefully, we'll never have to open up those boxes and actually sort them out.

Unfortunately, the reality tends to be different. Innately we all know that we're the only ones who can actually sort out our mental attic. Experience may also tell us that if we don't sort out the boxes ourselves, the contents will tend to jump out on us at some critical moment. It always happens at the very point we least want it too. Those nasty horrible things that we've been avoiding often present themselves in situations of high emotion. Inevitably, when we feel under most pressure or we're anxious about something. Our little boxes become trapdoors. Sometimes the boxes can contain powerful negative memories that we've been locking away. These in particular can almost become like explosive trapdoors or land mines.

In my experience, there is only one solution. We need to pull out the boxes, open them up and start to address and resolve whatever is inside them (Epstein, 1995; Allione, 2008). So far, I've found that the vast majority of issues centre around three elements – fear, anger and guilt. These tend to be the issues we need to resolve. We need to forgive ourselves for whatever we feel guilty about, or forgive others for whatever we feel angry about. We need to conquer whatever fears we have. Normally this involves some discomfort and usually takes courage (Gilbert, 2005). Usually it will involve admitting that we were wrong or accepting parts of our character that we might wish were different. It is our ego and our pride that feel the discomfort. They are the aspects of ourself that probably caused the issues in the first place. It is likely to have been our ego that felt guilty, angry or fearful, which we subsequently locked up in the boxes of our mental attic.

There is one huge benefit that we receive once we have cleared out our boxes. The process demands that we take responsibility (Martin-Fischer and Ravizza, 1998). If we are to truly resolve any of these issues, we must take responsibility. If we blamed someone else, we would simply not get to a point of resolution. Instead, we would simply be re-sealing the box (with all the nasty stuff still inside it) and putting it back in the attic. We stand the very real chance that we'd worsen the issue and make it all potentially more explosive by adding 'blame' into the mix. Blame tends to increase anger or guilt, rather than reduce it. These concepts are central to many methods used in psychotherapy (Sommers-Flanagan and Sommers-Flanagan, 2004).

By taking responsibility when we clear out our boxes, we start a process of taking responsibility as we go forwards. If we take responsibility and avoid blaming circumstances or other people, we will avoid creating new boxes and new trapdoors in the future. If we blame others or blame circumstance, we hand over control of our destiny.

Only when we take responsibility, can we take control (Martin Fischer and Ravizza, 1998; Koestenbaum and Block, 2001; Jauncey, 2002; Nesti, 2004). It is a fundamental element of producing peak performances. It is a trait that is common amongst true champions. Taking responsibility is a habit of the great performers.

Summary

- Take things at their own merit and see them for what they really are.
- Ensure that you have a broad and balanced life.
- Performance in one area does not dictate your success as a person.
- Our ego tends to create trapdoors. If we can put our ego to bed, the trapdoors tend to disappear.
- Sometimes we need to confront the things that are uncomfortable.

10

Habits of great performers

Great performers know that great performances don't happen by chance. They don't happen overnight and they can't be produced by the click of a finger. In his book, *Outliers*, Malcolm Gladwell (2008) explains that it takes over 10,000 hours of practice to become expert in something. He cites a number of examples, such as Mozart, The Beatles and Michael Phelps. However, the '10,000 hour rule', as it has been dubbed, could be applied to just about anything.

The 10,000 hour rule also supports the well-recognized idea that talent is actually a very poor predictor of performance. Geoff Colvin (2008) has written an entire book on the subject, called, *Talent is Overrated*. I would tend to agree. To me, someone who is talented is naturally gifted. Their natural gifts give them a starting point. The talent gives them potential, but it does not guarantee that they will fulfil that potential (Starkes and Ericsson, 2003; Farrow, Baker and MacMahon, 2007). Great performers may have talent, but they certainly don't rely on their talent. Over the last 15 years, I have worked with hundreds of athletes and players. Those athletes who are the most naturally gifted and talented are *not* the ones that have achieved the most. One of the Premiership football clubs I worked with had three exceptionally skilled players. In many people's opinion, two of them in particular were amongst the most talented that they'd ever seen. Interestingly, neither of them had any kind of work ethic.

Both players relied on their talent to get by. I suspect that their talent had been good enough to get them to that point (i.e. it had been enough to get them into a Premiership club). They hadn't needed to work particularly hard or stretch themselves, so they probably didn't see any need to change. Despite their talents, both players found it difficult to make a real impression or secure a regular first team slot. They often found themselves coming off the substitute's bench. Occasionally, they would produce a moment of extreme skill, but rarely did they make a significant impact. One of the players in particular was simply not physically fit enough (and wouldn't work hard enough to become fit), therefore he couldn't make a sustained impression on the games. Eventually, both players ended up leaving the club. They played in and around the top flight for a season or two but then disappeared. Arguably, neither of them realized their potential or made the most of their talent.

In comparison, there was a *no frills* central defender at the club who was, by his own admission, not the most talented footballer on Earth. He was (and still is) a very good professional. He works hard and is very diligent about his game. Although not supremely talented, he has absolutely made the most of the talent he has. Arguably, he has performed to his potential. Unlike the two naturally gifted players, our hard working professional is still playing Premiership football many years later.

I saw a very similar situation when working in Premiership rugby union. Our club had two fly-halves, both of whom were excellent players. Our first choice player was very professional. He worked incredibly hard at his game and was constantly looking for ways to improve. He would often be seen taking a bag of balls out of his car boot when everyone else was heading home after training. As many other players were hitting the golf course, or switching on their Play Stations, he would be practising. He would be in the gym early, sometimes on his own with the fitness trainer, and was often last to leave.

Our second choice fly-half was not lazy by any means. He did what he was asked to do and didn't cut corners. He was also arguably the more naturally talented of the two. However, he wasn't the first choice in his position. As a result he was often played out of position. Eventually he chose to leave the club in an attempt to become a first choice fly-half somewhere else. In reality, our first choice fly-half closed the talent gap between himself and his team-mate with sheer hard work.

These are not isolated examples. I'm sure you've seen many similar situations yourself. It is often the person (or team) who is willing to go the extra mile who will be the most successful. There are some who will disregard the tiny details, thinking they are unimportant or won't make any difference. Others will make sure they pick up on the tiny details and get them absolutely right. Many years ago I met a former Coarse Fishing World Champion. I listened to him explaining why one person can catch loads of fish, whilst the person sitting next to him catches almost nothing. He explained that there were a number of tiny details that only made a minute difference. In fact, there were a couple of dozen minute things that made a difference: for example, how neatly the hooks were tied, how thick the line was, how clean the bait was, how accurately the bait was presented to the fish. All these tiny details added up. The cumulative effect was that the fish would tend to choose one angler's bait over the other. The tiny details made the difference between winning a World Championship and not winning.

I often listen to the performance directors from Olympic sports talking about how they plan to gain a competitive advantage over the opposition. On one occasion, I listened to Stephen Park, the Olympic manager from the RYA (British Sailing team), explaining how the polish that they applied to the bottoms of the boats made a slight difference to the drag on the boat. The cost of finding, testing and sourcing the polish was considerable. The effect may have been relatively small, but nonetheless it was a detail he was determined to get right. I know that British Cycling and many other Olympic sports do the same. They know that ultimately a couple of per cent can make the difference between a World record and not even making the final. This dedication to attention to detail has been documented in a number of World Class sporting organizations (Gilson, Pratt, Roberts and Weymes, 2000).

Take a moment to think about your own performance. Do you chase down all the tiny details? Do you challenge yourself to get absolutely everything as close to perfect as possible? Are there things that you'd consider were 'too small to bother about'? Many people often ask how they can get an extra 10–20 per cent performance. The answer is usually pretty simple. If you find five to ten things that you can get an extra 1 or 2 per cent from, then you can find the 10–20 per cent you need. In the film *Any Given Sunday*, Al Pacino describes American Football as 'a game of inches'. To be successful you need to gain every single inch that you can. The trick is to add up all the inches. He points out that the inches we need are all around us. In his words, they are in 'every break of the game, every minute, every second'. That's true of life. The opportunities to gain 1 or 2 per cent by picking up the tiny details are all around us.

I often conduct an exercise with teams that helps us to identify what those tiny details are. I've given it a glitzy title (because I'm a performance coach and that's what we do) – 'Creating a World Class Vision'. I first did the exercise with one of the Great Britain Olympic squads. After talking with their coaches, it became apparent that most of the coaches and most of the athletes didn't actually know what was required to become genuinely World Class

Table 10.1 The 'World Class vision' of a Great Britain Olympic squad

Amateur	Professional	World Class
Not giving your all	Good organization	Always highly focused
No programme or plan	Good personal management	Takes on tough targets
Amateur lifestyle and diet	Consistently hits targets	Hunger and dedication
Forgets kit at times	Takes responsibility	No excuses
Goes through the motions	Trains well	Always wants to improve
Moans	Good attitude and will to win	Uses the team around them
Lack of preparation	Detailed plan and programme	Always high quality training
Takes short cuts	Records, monitors and reviews	Attends to tiny details
Lazy in training	Professional lifestyle	Always learning
Doesn't consider others	Professional diet	Never satisfied

and compete for medals in major competitions. They had a pattern and a programme that they followed. The results over the last few years clearly showed that their programme produced performances that were well outside of the medals. They needed to do things differently to change their results. They needed different processes. The exercise simply asked them to identify behaviours that they would consider were *amateur*, *professional* and *World Class*. What they came up with, in the athletes' words, is shown in Table 10.1. A slightly different example from an elite rowing crew is given in Table 10.2.

Once we had created the tables, we also discussed how the squads felt their current practice rated in each area. Was their current practice *amateur*, *professional* or *World Class*? Both squads were looking to win medals at world level, so by definition they needed to be World Class. Most of their responses suggested that they were amateur or

Table 10.2 The 'World Class vision' of an elite rowing squad

Amateur	Professional	World Class
Not caring in some sessions	Relishes doing sessions	Learns from everything!
Only performs when being watched	Can do it on their own	Is a role model
Falls apart under pressure	Performs when required	Questions everything
Doesn't understand the reason for sessions	Recognizes weaknesses and works on them	Self-critical and improves on their own
Disorganized	Efficient in training	Does great sessions in any circumstance
Assumes everything	Communicates well with coaches	Uses negatives to improve
Doesn't question their own progression		Consistent high quality
		Vacuum for knowledge

professional, so we identified ways in which they could change their practice and move towards being World Class.

As you can imagine, making these kinds of changes requires a great deal of effort. It requires them to enter their discomfort zone. The squads found that as they started to change their practices, the performances started to follow. Unsurprisingly, they found that the hard work started to translate into improved results when they adopted the phrase 'train like you compete and compete like you train'. Although it seems obvious, many athletes will prepare very differently for training and competition. They will save their best preparation for competition and employ their second best for training. The result is that they don't produce their best performances regularly in training. Common sense dictates that if you don't produce better and better performances in training, you will not produce them consistently in competition. What benefit is there in scrimping on the preparation for training sessions? The other obvious consequence is that training doesn't closely replicate the demands of competition. We don't adopt the same mindset or train ourselves to perform under true competition conditions. In a sense, they become two separate entities. This is also common sense. However, many performers are surprised that they find it difficult to transfer their 'form' in training over to competition (Taylor and Wilson, 2005).

Some of the world's greatest athletes have benefited from having an environment that constantly requires them to produce World Class performances. Over the years, there have been examples where a number of the world's best athletes have been pushing each other, sometimes on a daily basis. In the 1980s Great Britain had a group of middle-distance runners that included Seb Coe, Steve Cram, Steve Ovett and Tom McKean. This small group of athletes would regularly train and compete against each other and push each other to become better and better. They were amongst the very best in the world at the time. If they beat each other, the chances were that they would beat anyone else in the world. The same was true with the 2008 British Olympic Cycling team. The standard of the competition in training was second to none. In order to simply make the British team, athletes would have to be capable of breaking World Records. As a result, members of the team found themselves breaking records in qualifying rounds of the 2008 Olympics (Attwooll, 2008).

In the Beijing Olympic Games of 2008, Michael Phelps set a record for the number of gold medals won by a single Olympian in one Games. In his interviews, he mentioned a lesser known US swimmer called Ryan Lochte (Gonzalez, 2008). Although not as famous, Lochte has multiple Olympic medals, including gold medals from both 2004 and 2008. Michael Phelps credits swimmers such as Ryan Lochte for pushing him so hard. For Phelps, being challenged to beat Lochte on a regular basis almost guarantees that he is capable of beating anyone else in the world.

We don't need to be in an Olympic programme to be able to draw on that principle. There are opportunities to pitch ourselves against other great performers in our own fields. Great performers pitch themselves against other greats. They test themselves and challenge themselves. Sometimes this happens by chance. Sometimes it happens by design. Great performers will often deliberately find an opponent who can expose their weaknesses or challenge them. For example, tennis players may pitch themselves against left-handed players or players with an awkward serve because it presents them with a tough challenge. A middle-distance runner might pitch himself against fast finishers if that is one of his weaker areas. Athletes may not get their ideal challenge dropped onto their laps. Often they go hunting for them.

Great performers make sure that their challenges always become more difficult. I often describe this as a set of hurdles that only ever get higher. There is almost no point in challenging yourself to clear a hurdle that you could manage with your eyes shut. If they are to work for us and make us better, they have to get higher. Inevitably, when we challenge ourselves with higher hurdles, we create the possibility (and probability) that we will hit some. The great performers I've seen are not scared of hitting hurdles. One of their greatest single qualities is the ability to get up and go again. In fact, I have often noticed that the very best performers are those who have experienced the hurdles and the bumps in the road – 'The harder you work, the harder it is to surrender' (Vince Lombardi).

A few years ago I worked with two swimmers. Both were Internationals in their events. They were both very professional, had a great attitude and worked exceptionally hard on their performance. In fact they were similar in many ways. The big difference between them was their life circumstances. One had a pretty cozy life. He lived in a flat that his parents provided him with. He was very comfortable and his lifestyle was designed to allow him to focus his energies on competing and training with very few other worries. There were very few bumps in his road. By comparison, the other swimmer's journey was dominated by bumps. He didn't have the same lifestyle or luxuries and needed to take care of himself. Money was tight, life was less comfortable and he had to make the best of it. The second swimmer often found that he had to work in imperfect conditions, find solutions and think on his feet. As you can imagine, these challenges made him stronger. He became very adept at producing very high quality performances in imperfect conditions. He was used to dealing with problems and was un-phased by the bumps in the road. The first swimmer of course didn't have the benefit of this experience. Whenever he encountered the bumps, it became a major issue for him. He found it difficult to perform in imperfect conditions and became flustered more easily. Although many people would advocate removing the bumps in the road, I actually think it's better to have them and use them. In many ways, removing the challenges is artificial.

No doubt, you will have witnessed exactly the same outside of sport. Whether in business or life, often those who succeed are those who had to fight to get where they are. The very process of fighting is likely to have helped them to achieve. Many great entrepreneurs have started life in what would normally be considered a 'disadvantaged' position. If you examine the life stories of many of today's business leaders, they started out with nothing (Kilpatrick, 2003; Caan, 2009; Sugar, 2010). Maybe that 'disadvantage' is in fact an advantage? Perhaps it is a disadvantage to have the trappings of a comfort zone? It is possible that the environment that many successful entrepreneurs were brought up in focused them to become successful. It presented them with the challenges and the lessons they needed in order to be successful.

It is true that great performers are incredibly focused. The great athletes I have worked with know exactly what they need to do in every single session. They know that each session is valuable and that they need to extract every ounce of possible benefit from it. One day I chatted to an Olympian about his sessions for the day. He told me that in his twelve-week training cycle, today was only one of eight sessions that was specifically focused on increasing his top speed. The other sessions focused on other elements such as endurance, technique or starts. In his mind, this session was crucial. If he missed the opportunity, he only had another seven sessions to increase his top speed before his major competition at the end of the year. He also lived by the philosophy that if he became 0.1 per cent better in every session, by the end of the week he'd be almost 1 per cent better. By the end of the training cycle, he could be 10 per cent better.

This philosophy is so simple, and yet it applies to almost every area of life. If we focus and apply ourselves to everything we do, we will start to do it a little better. If we make tiny improvements on every occasion, those improvements will add up over time. Great performances don't happen by chance. They don't happen overnight or by the click of a finger (Colvin, 2008). We don't tend to make huge leaps towards our goals; we tend to take steps. Great performers work on making a continual series of very focused but normally quite small steps. They do this very deliberately, and in doing so they take responsibility for their development and their performances.

I often see a very distinct divide between those who take responsibility for their performance and those who don't. Usually those who don't take responsibility get frustrated much more easily. Although it sounds easier to blame others, the fact is that if we fail to take responsibility we also fail to take control (Martin Fischer and Ravizza, 1998; Koestenbaum and Block, 2001; Nesti, 2004). In order to have control over our performance we must accept responsibility and be accountable for it (Jauncey, 2002). Only then can we have any control. Do you remember our fencing squad back in the Introduction? Their mindset and therefore their performances were being controlled by everyone else and everything else because they had not taken responsibility for them. By taking responsibility, we must accept that whatever situation we find ourselves in, we have created it. This can sometimes be tough. I know this from personal experience.

I have found myself working very hard on projects that have failed to produce the results. The temptation sometimes is to look at the hard work that I've put in and conclude that the project's failure is somehow due to circumstance. It's more comfortable in the short term to put it all down to 'bad luck' or other people's failure to deliver. In reality though, the responsibility is mine. Only when I recognize this will I be able to learn from it. If I can't see the mistakes I made, I won't be able to correct them and I run the risk of doing the same thing next time and the time after that. That could get disheartening. However, if I accept responsibility, I will start looking for the reasons behind the results. Did I back a project without knowing it was definitely viable? Did I research it well enough before we started? Did I give responsibility to others without knowing that they could deliver? Did I leave some elements of the project's success to chance? The answer of course is that I made mistakes. If I recognize that I am responsible, I can start working on these issues so that I can adapt my approach next time. If I fail to recognize the mistakes because I choose to blame circumstances, I will never make the changes I need to make.

The vast majority of what we need to learn comes from self-coaching (Luciani, 2004). I use this phrase deliberately. Some say that experience is the greatest teacher, but I'd tend to disagree. Experience gives you an opportunity to learn. Some take full advantage of the opportunity, whereas others don't. The reality is that we have to be our own teachers and coaches. Ultimately, great performers often are their own coaches. Not only do they learn from their own experiences, but they actively seek out the knowledge that they need. They are true students of their chosen field. The great athletes, coaches and managers that I've worked with are genuine students of their sport. Great business leaders are students of business and of their industries. They have a thirst for knowledge. Their passion drives them to find out what they don't know and to understand what they don't fully understand. They constantly question and challenge the norm – 'Question everything. Learn something. Answer nothing' (Euripides, Greek playwright, c. 480–406 BC).

Many elite athletes and executives that I've worked with have a habit of questioning. They rarely take an answer or a solution at face value. Often they will look deeper. They are keen to see whether there is a better way of doing things. They are constantly looking for improvements and refinements. As a result, they become innovators (Weisberg, 2006). This doesn't mean that they are looking to re-invent the wheel. It means that they are constantly raising the bar. They push themselves and everyone else around them to become better. This habit is something that would probably be classed as a quality of good management.

Many of the Olympians that I worked with began to evolve into managers. This may seem bizarre when you consider that the majority were 'individual athletes'. Why would a swimmer, a runner or a gymnast need to become a good manager? The answer is quite simple. Top athletes operate like many other high performers. They surround themselves with experts (Bannatyne, 2006). Typically, a top Olympian will have coaches, a sport psychologist, medics, a physiologist, a performance analyst and a strength and conditioning coach. Each of these experts will give feedback and input into the training programme, preparation strategy and performance reviews. The athlete then has the task of ensuring that they manage their team, so that the team delivers. They need to become adept at drawing what they need from their team. Not only must the athlete start to coordinate their team of experts, but they must also push that team to raise the bar. Great athletes encourage their teams to become critical in all areas and to keep searching for the extra 1 per cent that will provide a performance gain. The team needs to share the athlete's vision and be able to dedicate themselves to helping the athlete achieve their goals.

This of course is common in other arenas. Managers in all fields often strive to do the same. They need to engage their teams and ensure that they get absolutely the best from each of the individuals (Jauncey, 2002). They push to ensure that their processes become better and better. Whilst working with one particular business I was often heard saying to the team: 'it's very good, but it's not World Class yet'. Although it may sound pernickety, our aim was not to become very good. The aim of the business was to become World Class in our field. In order to do that, we needed to start with very high standards and keep increasing them. We developed a *never satisfied mindset*, which is common amongst truly great performers, whether they be athletes, executives, surgeons or teachers. Many of the genuinely World Class athletes that I've worked with often score themselves as a 6/10 in their performances. It's ironic that many juniors will score themselves as a 9/10. Although it may seem unusual at first glance, the reason is quite straightforward. The World Class athlete is acutely aware of all of the areas they can still improve on. They have a great appreciation of the fine details and see the gap between 9.9/10 and 10/10. It is no coincidence that athletes who have this appreciation go on to become World Class. Their awareness of the imperfections drives them to continually work on their game.

The almost obsessive strive for perfection can sometimes be a double-edged sword. Striving for perfection is clearly a significant factor in becoming a great performer. However, many people can become almost neurotic about their performance. Their life becomes completely dominated by it and they can lose their sense of perspective. We discussed the trapdoors that can appear when our life becomes so focused on the performance that we lose sight of everything else (Ben-Shahar, 2009). Jonny Wilkinson (2008) described his experiences of this challenge in his book, *Tackling Life: Striving for Perfection.* His accounts show that the quest for perfection can often be a very lonely and miserable one if your life is entirely devoted to one thing. It highlights the need for a balanced life and a broad sense of self, which we discussed in the previous chapter.

One way to achieve this is simply to focus on improving constantly, rather than perfecting. Although we need to be aware of the imperfections, we also need to focus on the improvement. Great performers in all disciplines are aware that the secret to producing a great performance is simple. The vast majority of great performers, whether they are organizations, teams or individuals, stick to a very simple rule. They do the basics exceptionally well (Gilson et al., 2000). Great performers sometimes do extra-ordinary things. However, the bulk of what they do is to deliver the basics better than anyone else. If you analyze the world's best athletes and sports teams, they often don't seem to have any magical formula. They don't do anything vastly different from their opponents. Instead, they do essentially the same things, but better. The great performers might be more precise, more consistent or be able to maintain the quality of their performance for longer. They may have practised their skills at a higher intensity, with less time or space available to them. Good coaches know that the performance we see in competition is usually lower than that on the training field, because the demands of competition are higher. Therefore, they need to raise the standard of the practice significantly in order to deliver a high standard on match day. Good coaches also know that there is no point in doing anything else until their team has absolutely mastered the basics first. And once they have absolutely mastered the basics, there is not much else to do.

I often see competitors fall apart because their opponent simply delivers the basics exceptionally well. Racket sports in particular illustrate this for me. I noticed an interesting pattern developing when I worked with the squash girls (Hartley, 2010g, 2011). I would watch a point being played out. Often one player would play a consistent series of very accurate and precise shots. Normally these would be played into an area of the court that caused their opponents the most challenges – on a squash court, this tended to be the back corners. After a while, the other player would start looking for ways to break the status quo and get out of the corners. Invariably they would start playing riskier shots. The player who played consistently precise shots would then start stretching their opponent, so that the opponent's shots became weaker and provided them with opportunities to play a winner. The cumulative effect of consistently accurate shots started to take effect. After a while, the player on the receiving end would start making forced errors when they took more risky shots – shots that were not really on. Following a couple of forced errors, the frustration would start to set in. Not long after that, we would then see the unforced errors. As you can probably imagine, unforced errors lead to further frustration and the game starts to crumble (Crust and Nesti, 2006).

The same pattern can be seen quite clearly in a variety of sports. When batsmen in cricket feel that they need to score runs, they will often play risky shots and therefore stand a much greater chance of getting themselves out. Equally, if bowlers feel that they desperately need a wicket, they may bowl more erratically and therefore stand more chance of giving away runs. The same decisions can be seen throughout sports. Quarter backs in the NFL throw more interceptions when they are continually denied time and space, or when they need yards to make a first down. Often it takes a great deal of resolve to avoid forcing plays that aren't there. When the game starts to go against them, I often see teams throw the game plan out of the window and start playing off the cuff.

To me, one definition of mental strength is to stick to your game plan, whatever happens. This principle is recognized outside of sport. Mark Douglas applies the same mindset to trading on the stock exchange (Douglas, 2000). So often, individuals and teams forget the game plan completely when they are asked some serious questions. Often they don't have enough knowledge of the game plan or enough confidence in it. Many people ask me why it is that champion teams can always seem to nick a win at the last minute. Why is it that they always win by a narrow margin rather than lose? Perhaps it is that they have absolute faith in their game plan and their ability to execute it? As a result, they keep delivering all of their processes until the very last minute. Maybe their opposition starts to crumble and starts to waver in the face of this, and consequently abandons their game plan at the last minute? It is true that sometimes tactics need changing. However, a change of tactics should be a part of the overall game plan. It should be something that has been practised, rehearsed and stress tested so that it is second nature.

In 2006, Great Britain's Chris Cook won the 100 metres breaststroke final at the Commonwealth Games. He turned fifth at the half-way point. As he turned, he knew that he'd delivered his first 50 metres according to his game plan. He didn't worry. He didn't change his game plan. Chris knew that he had a very specific game plan, which was designed for him and drew on his individual strengths. The game plan was his. In fact, it probably would not have suited anyone else in the race. Chris was so confident in his plan that he simply kept delivering it until he hit the wall to finish. As a result, he took home the gold medal.

One of the reasons why Chris found it so easy to stick to the plan is that he knew it was his. It was very personal to him. It was authentic. We hadn't adapted it from someone else's game plan or copied it. The race plan was created by Chris for Chris. We could only do this because Chris knew himself. He knew himself and could therefore be himself. He had the confidence in himself as a person and an athlete. This confidence allowed him to be himself and deliver his performance. As far as I am concerned, this is probably the single greatest attribute of a World Class performer. It allows them to keep things really simple and stick to their very simple job. Authenticity goes hand in hand with true success. Only when we know ourselves, accept ourselves and allow ourselves to be authentic can we truly deliver great performances (Frankl, 1959/1984; Csikszentmihalyi, 1990; Orlick, 1998; Seligman, 2005).

Summary

- Great performers are often not the most naturally gifted.
- Often the great performers are those who go the extra mile and get the tiny details right.
- Continually test yourself and push to become better. Look for higher hurdles and tougher challenges.
- When you take responsibility, you take control.
- Be yourself.

11

Coaching others to achieve peak performances

I left school with an A grade in GCSE Mathematics, so I confidently packed my bags and went off to college to study it at A Level. A couple of weeks into the course, I found that Maths was all of a sudden much more difficult. I sat in a classroom with many other successful GCSE students, but we just didn't seem to understand anything. Our lecturer would set us a series of tasks (normally from the trusty textbook) and we would have a go at them. Inevitably our answers were incorrect, so our lecturer would show us what we'd done wrong and set us another series of exercises to try. We repeated this pattern a lot. I honestly felt no wiser going into the exam room at the end of two years than I did on Day One. Consequently I was one of the 70 per cent of my class who came out with an *ungraded* mark (a fail) at the end of my course. Some of the class did reach the heady heights of an E or a D grade, but the vast majority of us didn't quite get that far.

At the time, the experience didn't strike me as being very useful. I felt like I'd wasted two years of my life on the subject. However, a few years later I started to see the same patterns again in a different situation. This time I saw it in a football dressing room. The manager would sit the players down at half time and explain to them where they were going wrong. He'd then send them out for the second half and was always amazed that they didn't simply go out and put things right. I used to see the constant frustration in the manager, which reminded me of my Maths lecturer. Both the manager and my lecturer had made the same mistake. They assumed that pointing out the errors would automatically lead to the solution. The fact is, as human beings, we often need more than that. Understanding where we went wrong is fine, but it is not enough. We also need to know how we should be performing and we need to be able to practise it. Practising is absolutely crucial if we're going to change our performance.

Often the manager would ask the team to change their tactics or their formation on the field to counter what the opposition was doing. The problem was, our players hadn't practised doing that. They'd never played in the formation before or practised the new tactics. It was not simply a case of switching to something they knew and were confident in. Therefore, they tried it initially, found that it didn't work very well and reverted back to what they did know. As the manager moaned at them for making the same mistakes time after time, the players' confidence started to drain away. The players (just like our Maths class) didn't know what to do or how to do it.

It's not just football managers (or Maths lecturers) who fall into this pattern. I'm sure you will have seen it, been on the receiving end of it or maybe even fallen into it yourself at some point. So, what's the alternative? How do we turn around performances, undo negative spirals, start positive spirals and change our results?

I will try to explain this using a real-life example of a professional football team in the UK. We'll take it step by step and I'll show you the process we used to turn around its performance. At the start of the process the team was losing, the strikers had become shot-shy, confidence was ebbing away and the squad had started to argue, blame each other and moan. Morale was pretty low. So where did we start?

It might sound obvious but we need to start at the beginning. We started from zero. Step 1 is to clarify and simplify. Firstly, we need to ensure that everyone understands their job in the simplest possible terms. If we're working in a team, we need to know the job of the team. What is its reason to exist? What does it need to do to be successful and achieve its targets?

In our football team it was pretty simple. Let's get right back to basics. We're trying to score more goals than the opposition, which means that we need to score more and concede less. Everyone in the team has a role to play in these two jobs. Every player needs to know their role in simple clear terms (Bray and Brawley, 2002a, 2002b). When we started the exercise with the coaching staff, I asked what each player's role was in those jobs. Their answers were a little woolly to start with. The fact is that if the coaching staff weren't clear, how would the players be clear? After a little work, we started to clarify each and every person's role and what we needed from them.

Now that we know the job, and we have clarified the roles for each person, we can set about putting Stage 2 into place and start building confidence. One of the fundamental strategies to build confidence is to start with the things people can do well. Therefore, as part of this exercise I was keen to know how we could help the players by making their jobs as easy as possible.

At the football club, we spent a long time looking through the video footage of the matches. The club already had a great deal of performance analysis data and clips of the players that were catalogued. This allowed us to pick out all the instances where the players performed well and all of those in which the players struggled. Once we had these, we looked for patterns. One of the centre forwards in particular struggled in certain positions on the field. He also struggled when he was asked to receive certain types of passes. When we analyzed the overall footage, we found that he was forced to play to his weaknesses for the majority of the game. However, there were instances when he looked extremely comfortable, effective and dangerous. Again, there were patterns. He was most effective in specific areas of the field and when he could receive short, fast, accurate passes. So, we needed to change the way the team played slightly in order to help this player become more effective.

Once we had the information on one player, we could also find out how the others played at their best. We could see when they were most comfortable and most effective. We could also see where they struggled and when their weaknesses were being exposed. Gradually we built up a picture of the squad and started to form a game plan that drew on their strengths. We then set about putting this into practice on the training field. Gradually, we increased the intensity and the demands so that our practice became like competition. This built up so that, eventually, the challenges we set in practice surpassed the demands of competition.

Even though we need to start building confidence by focusing on the things our people can do, we also need to progress by working on those things they are not so good at. There will be weaknesses that people need to work hard on, so that they can become confident in those areas.

We put this into action in the football club by structuring each player's practice so that they gradually became more and more confident in the areas they previously struggled with. Obviously, this doesn't happen overnight. Not only do they need to practice, but they need to test themselves in competitive situations. The players and coaches know that learning requires time and mistakes, so as much of this as possible is done on the training field rather than on match day. Once they're comfortable and confident, they'll start to bring more into competitive games. Realistically, we know that it won't be perfect and that there will always be mistakes and learning at this stage.

If we have made solid progress with the first few steps we should have started the positive spiral. In order to build the confidence, we will need to ensure that we're evaluating honestly and objectively. We need to focus on the performance and the process, not the results. Normally there is a delay between the performance improvement and the corresponding change in results.

At the football club, we were conscious that each player had a very clear job and that they should be evaluated against that job. The coaching staff were very careful to make sure that their feedback was evaluative (rather than judgemental), honest, objective and focused on the delivery of that player's job. There was no room for blame or excuses. Everyone was charged with taking responsibility for their role and delivering it to the best of their ability. Win, lose or draw, we needed to stick to this process.

This same process can be used in larger organizations. I have recently been working with a number of businesses, helping them to increase their performance. We start by simplifying and clarifying. I normally use the *2 Lengths of the Pool* analogy that we discussed in Chapter 3. With an organization, the first stage is to understand the job of the organization in the simplest possible terms. We need to find out what their *2 Lengths* is. This normally takes time. I am always amazed at the variety of responses I get from board members of the same company when I ask them to describe the organization's job.

When we know the *2 Lengths* for the organization, we can then start to define the jobs for each group, team and department within the business. As we do this, we must ensure that the job for every team is aligned with the overall *2 Lengths* for the organization. Each team needs to contribute fully to the organization. We need to know that if each team delivers its job, the organization will be successful in its job.

This exercise is then cascaded down through the organization so that each individual knows their own job in the simplest possible terms (Donnelly and Ivancevich, 1975). Everyone should know their own *2 Lengths*, as well as that of their team and the organization as a whole. Everyone should also be able to see how their job contributes to their team and ultimately to the organization. When we have this alignment within the organization, we have the foundations.

Once we have those foundations in place, we will be able to add newer, greater and more demanding challenges. We can start to raise the bar and start to really enter the discomfort zone. Gradually, we can ask our people to start pushing their boundaries. We can start picking up on the fine details. We can start looking for better delivery and more consistency in more demanding situations. We can raise the targets and the standards.

This is a process that has been used to good effect in some Olympic sports. A number of Olympic performance directors in the UK took the bold step of setting a new standard for athletes to achieve (Harris, 2009). One in particular made it clear that there was no point in having athletes on the programme if they didn't have genuine medal-winning prospects. Therefore, in order to get on the programme and receive any funding, every athlete needed to be producing World Class times in their events. The bar was set. Let's imagine the process. Initially, the athletes need to get into the top 12 in the world. It is a tough challenge but many of them work hard and achieve it. They take a sigh of relief. They are in the programme and have secured their funding. Then the bar rises. Now the athletes need to be in the top 10, so they push themselves again. As before, many make it. Phew! I'm sure you're ahead of me already. That's right, once they make the top 10 the bar rises again to the top 8, and finally the top 6.

So, how did the coaches help those athletes continually make the improvements necessary to get over that rising bar? The formula is pretty straightforward. As a coach you need to set a 'plan, do and review' process into play. I use a system called performance profiling as a structure (Hartley, 2007) and it's embarrassingly simple. We outlined the basic principles in Chapter 5.

A performance profile helps us to understand the key elements of a performance. When I profile with an athlete I will start by asking them to identify the most important elements of their performance. Normally we limit this to around eight things, although I prefer around five. These elements have to be those that have the biggest impact on their performance. When the athlete gets these five to eight things right, a peak performance is almost guaranteed. In Chapter 3, we outlined the *5 Keys*. These 5 Keys would be a perfect starting point. To be honest, this part of the exercise alone is worth its weight in gold. It helps the athlete to really understand what drives their performance and what makes a difference to them.

Once we have these five to eight elements, I ask the athlete to start rating themselves using a scale of 1–10. A score of 10 equates to an absolutely perfect performance every single time in that specific element. When I conduct this exercise with athletes or executives, I often challenge and stress test the scores to make sure they are justified. This also helps me to understand the athlete's experience in more detail. For example, if a long jumper rated his approach to the board as a 6/10, it's useful to know why. It might be because he feels that the run-up gets choppy towards the end, or that the stride pattern needs changing. Understanding the reason of course helps us to make improvements to that element.

Now that we have a score for each element, we can start to set targets and strategies to improve each area. Very simply, I ask the athlete and their coach how they can close the gap between their current level of performance and their target level. We talk through their strategies and the training plan. At this stage, I also ask the athlete to describe the differences between their current level and their target. For example, if they are a 6/10 today and they have a target to get to 8/10 in 6 weeks, we need to know what an 8/10 will look like. How will we know when we get there? What will we see, hear or feel that is different? How will the athlete think, act and talk when they are an 8/10? We need to create a meaning behind the number. I also tend to chat to the athlete about the difference that those two points will make to their performance. We discuss the benefits of getting this element to 8/10 and what impact it is likely to have on their performance. This helps the athlete really start to understand the reasons for working on this element and the importance of making the changes.

The performance profile starts to give us a structure for the athlete's development and a mechanism to review progress. Because it is so simple and yet so effective, I have used performance profiling with a huge variety of performers, from show jumpers to sales people. It is an incredibly versatile tool and I suspect that it can be used to help increase human performance in any field.

A few years ago I worked with a sales team in a training company. The company provided a range of National Vocational Qualifications (NVQ)-based courses for learners in the workplace. The business was paid on the number of learners who signed up and then completed their courses. Therefore, the sales people were charged with signing up as many learners as possible. They did this by engaging the employers first, in order to gain access to their staff. Once the employer was on board, the sales team aimed to attract as many learners as possible onto their courses.

The courses were free to both the employer and the learner because the government paid the bill. It was a fairly simple model and theoretically easy to sell, but the sales team were finding it hard to consistently hit their targets.

We started a project to help the five-man sales team to hit their targets month on month. We used a performance profile with each of the sales executives. Table 11.1 is an example of a profile from the most senior member of the team. He has identified his *5 Keys to Success* and started to understand what each element needed to look like (in the 'Vision' column). In addition, he has scored each area, created a target for 6 weeks time and has a strategy. In summary, the senior sales executive concluded that he needs to spend more time on his biggest accounts and he needs to be on site more whilst the programme is being delivered. This will mean that he can ensure the delivery is done well and that the customer is happy throughout the process. He can then focus on generating referral business rather than using 'cold leads', as he termed them. In his view, this will make him more effective and give him the best chance of consistently hitting the target.

We used this structure throughout the 6-week support programme to review his progress and to discuss aspects that were working well and areas that needed to be refined. We worked to a very simple process – plan, do and review. At the end of the 6 weeks, each of the areas of the performance profile had progressed. In some areas he had reached his target and the other areas were well on their way. As a result, the sales executive had become much more effective and was starting to see the resultant change in his sales figures.

This simple process was mirrored in the other four members of the team. By improving their effectiveness and enhancing their processes, each team member started to generate more sales. Their processes became more consistent, which was reflected in their results. In addition, we

Table 11.1 The performance profile of a sales director

Element	Vision	Current Rating	Target	Strategy
Manage time	• Prioritize • Understand what's most effective	7.5/10	9.5/10	• Spend more time on bigger projects (do 3 major accounts rather than 10 smaller ones)
Sales pitch	• Understand what the customer needs and structure the pitch to deliver it	8.5/10	9.9/10	• Keep evolving and refining pitch by increasing knowledge and remaining current and up to date • Discuss customer needs in more detail and listen
Information flow from me	• More effective flow in and out • Make sure I provide the right details • Make sure there is a solid process	7.5/10	9.5/10	• Create an internal process • Tick list and timescales
Ask clients for recommendations and referrals	• Need to have the confidence that we will deliver a great product	6/10	9/10	• Client management • Need to be involved in the process on site
Knowledge of the qualifications and how they're delivered	• Understand the products in complete detail • Know their life from beginning to end	7/10	9/10	• Visit accounts when the work is being delivered • Ensure solid delivery • Focus time on the bigger accounts

began to identify areas that could be improved within the overall business, and started to reduce some of the barriers that were hindering the sales team. We started to identify gaps in the Knowledge, Skills, Resources and Desire (KSRD) within the team and put strategies in place to plug those gaps. The overall effect was a steady rise in sales.

As you can see, the performance profile is an extremely simple tool that helps us to continually raise the bar and improve performance. However, the performance profile is not a magic wand. In order to make it work, we need to invest time, energy and focus into making the changes. All too often, I have seen coaches use the performance profile to *plan* but they fail to follow up with the *do* or *review*. In order to work, we need to employ the *plan*, the *do* and the *review*. All three are crucial. Without a plan, we're unlikely to get very far. If we don't *do*, we're not going to see any progress either. Most people will employ the first stage and possibly the second. However, the review is equally important but often forgotten.

Let's imagine we used a 'plan, do and review' process when we learned to walk. What would happen if we only planned? We might think about how we'll attempt to stand up. We might even identify some handy items that we could use to help us get up, such as the bars of the play pen or the coffee table. If that were all we did, we'd never actually stand up. We could go a stage further and attempt to execute our plan. We could grab hold of the bars of the play pen and try to pull ourselves up. It might work, it might not. If that is where the exercise ends, we are not going to learn how to walk. Even if we're successful in our attempt to stand, it will probably only last a little while before we plop back down.

The real power comes when we start reviewing and then start the cycle again (Graue, 2006). If we start to process the feedback and start to learn, we stand a great chance of being more successful next time. We can use our review to inform our next round of planning. In doing so, we gradually refine our approach and get better. The review process is the vital link and gives us the momentum that keeps the process going. Once the reviews stop, normally the process starts to fizzle out and our performance hits a plateau.

As we use this model, and start to improve our performance, we can start to look at ever more demanding challenges. We encourage the performers to step into their discomfort zone. Often we find new questions that we have not been asked before and therefore not answered before. The more critical we are, the more questions we find. As we begin to answer the questions, we often start to become creative and innovative. If we are still using our 'plan, do and review' process, our reviews will ensure that we learn throughout these periods.

During my career, I have worked with a lot of individuals who were not incredibly talented but were incredibly successful. I noticed something in all of them that was not so apparent in the more talented individuals. Those less-talented people had taken a journey. They started out with their dream of becoming successful and they worked and learned through the years until they found success. They knew every step of the journey. Their journey had given them a road map and a blueprint. This map showed them exactly how to become successful and the elements that are required. When they were experiencing a low point, these people could use their road map to show them the route back to their peak performance. Because they had taken the journey, and they knew the steps along the way, they were able to re-trace their steps. The talented performers often didn't have that road map. Many of them simply arrived at their destination. They just appeared on a world stage because they were talented. They didn't have the same journey, experiences or the lessons. Therefore, when they experienced lows, they had no route plan and couldn't re-trace their steps.

This process is as true for the coach as it is for the performer. As coaches, we have to recognize that we're on our own journey (Ayers, 2001). We don't have all the answers. As we step into our discomfort zones, we will also find new questions that we've never answered before. Some coaches shy away from these situations. Some like to think they have all the answers, so they stick to giving answers they are comfortable with regardless of whether they are the best answers or not. As we gain expertise, we go through waves of having questions, then having some answers and then having more questions again. As we understand more, we become increasingly aware of the things we still don't understand – 'The more I know, the more I realize I don't know' (Anon).

As any good coach knows, it all starts with ourself. If you want to help other people to perform, the starting point is you. People follow people. If you believe, there is a good chance that others will believe. If you don't believe, it's unlikely that others will believe. I've often seen coaches and managers who are nervous before big events. I remember seeing one football manager in particular who was extremely nervous before a 'big match'. He felt pressure, because he had got the job wrong. He thought that he needed to win the game. Winning meant promotion to the higher league and a huge increase in money and profile. The manager saw it as a big game because he was focusing on the outcome. He could only see the enormous difference between winning and losing. He was nervous, so his players were nervous. As human beings we are pretty good at detecting other people's moods, and so the manager's nerves started to rub off onto everyone else (Zanna, 2009). The end result was that the players didn't perform on the day and they lost their 'big game'. Unlike the manager, you don't have to be nervous and so your team doesn't have to be nervous either.

Fortunately, your performance is entirely within your control. Your performance is not dictated by anyone else or anything else. It's not dictated by circumstances or external factors. Your performance emanates from your thoughts and your feelings. Nobody can influence your thoughts or feelings, unless you let them! No situation or circumstance can impact on your thoughts or feelings, unless you allow it. You have ultimate control over how you think and feel, therefore you have ultimate control over your performance (Glasser, 1999).

You now have the tools necessary to control your confidence, master your motivation and hone your focus. You will also have a range of other strategies that are used by great performers. You know the habits of great performers and the trapdoors that others fall down. Using these strategies, you can now start to engineer your own performance and the performances of the people around you.

Peak performance no longer has to be left to chance. You can now ensure that you produce peak performances every time.

Summary

- Start with clarity and simplicity.
- Build on what you can do, play to your strengths and work on your weaknesses.
- Plan – Do – Review. It is simple and incredibly effective.
- Be constantly aware of how you can improve.
- Remember, you have ultimate control of your thoughts and feelings, therefore you have ultimate control over your performance.

Theoretical background and further reading

The purpose of this book is to provide very tangible and practical guidance on how to achieve peak performances consistently. It draws on my experiences as a practicing sport psychologist and performance coach and from my work with athletes, executives, sports teams, corporations, charities and education. Therefore, the methods and approaches contained in this book are grounded in real-world experience and real life. There is a great deal of research and theoretical background that underpins the work. However, the approaches are not grounded in theory. They were not borne out of the theory. In short, this book does not show how theory has been applied, but rather how real-world practice is underpinned by the theory. It would be true to say that I have been influenced, guided and even inspired by some of the literature that is cited here. However, there is no single theoretical approach or paradigm. My approach to practice is influenced by a range of theories and methods. Some of these have reasonably obvious links and overlaps with each other. Most are complementary. However, some may actually appear to conflict with each other theoretically.

I also take the view that theories are simply ways of trying to conceptualize the world and make sense of it. As humans, we love to find patterns and attach rules to phenomena. That's what science does. However, research and the theoretical perspectives that are generated from it are often the subject of interpretation. They are conceived by people who bring their experiences, views and perspectives with them. Often researchers and academics start to favour certain approaches and theoretical models over others. As a result, academic literature contains many discussions about the merits of one theory over another. I have no interest in engaging in the academic debates, or to critically appraise the merits of the various theories or research studies.

From a personal perspective, as a student I was influenced by a lecturer who had an appreciation of existential approaches. I found that existential methods resonated with me. I was also taught to take a broad view of the discipline of psychology, and to recognize the range of paradigms and approaches. This experience helped me to understand that sport psychology is dominated by cognitive-behavioural approaches. I would argue that focusing on one approach alone provides quite a narrow and limited view. The purpose of this book is to help you to enhance your performance and that of others. I believe that there are some very valuable approaches that lie beyond the boundaries of mainstream, cognitive-behavioural, sport psychology. Therefore, much of the theoretical underpinning here comes from approaches such as existentialism, humanistic psychology, positive psychology, Jungian psychology, neuroscience, coaching, personal development, education, business, management, philosophy and even spirituality. The bibliography includes some very notable academics, and also authors who write almost purely from their experience. The references that are used within this book are there to signpost you to further reading, should you wish to delve deeper. There are some targeted pieces of research in specific areas, plus some background texts on the underpinning theories, as well as some practical literature that may help you to apply some of the methods yourself. The aim of this chapter is not to debate these; it is simply to give you a little more background, and outline some of these resources in a little more detail.

There are some central themes that run throughout the book and underpin most of the approaches used. I will discuss these themes first. Then, there are some topic-specific approaches that also have theoretical underpinning and deserve attention.

Central themes

The central themes revolve around a number of fundamental principles.

We have ultimate control over our performance because we have ultimate control over how we think and feel

This central principle is supported by approaches in both philosophy and psychology. Concepts such as *free will*, *choice* and *responsibility* are at the heart of existentialism. Existentialism is based on the notion that, as human beings, we have both the freedom and responsibility to live a fulfilling life. As humans, we have both the power and responsibility to choose how we experience the world. In fact, existentialists would argue that freedom and responsibility are inseparable, and bound together because we have choice. We may not choose our circumstances, but ultimately our choices govern our lived experience. These principles are central to the works of authors such as Rollo May (1994), Ilman Dilman (1999), John Martin-Fischer and Martin Ravizza (1998), Ronald Valle and Steen Halling (1989) and Peter Koestenbaum and Peter Block (2001). Ernesto Spinelli (1996) presents a good outline of existential approaches to psychology. Rollo May, who was president at Saybrook Graduate School in San Francisco, writes from an existential psychological perspective, but has also been influenced by humanistic and Freudian approaches. Ilman Dilman is Professor Emeritus of Philosophy at the University of Wales and writes on philosophical psychology and existentialism. By contrast, Peter Koestenbaum held a professorship in philosophy at San José State University for over 30 years before focusing on applying his knowledge to leadership development. Charles Manz (2000, 2002), Professor of Leadership at the University of Massachusetts, also applies philosophy to business consultancy and management. Therefore, both Koestenbaum and Manz offer a more applied perspective on existential approaches. William Glasser (1999) is a psychiatrist who presents Choice Theory. Although Glasser's theory comes from a cognitive-behavioural background, it also suggests that the only person whose behaviour we can control is our own; other people control themselves. Glasser also draws on many of Abraham Maslow's (1998) humanistic principles.

The existential views on freedom, responsibility and choice are extended through the concept of *authenticity*. This book provides numerous illustrations of the need to be ourselves in order to perform at our peak. For example, if we are worried about what other people think of us, or how we might be judged, we often fail to perform at our peak. Existentialists would also argue that authenticity, being yourself, is crucial if we are to lead a fulfilled life. This principle is central to the work of Rollo May and many other existential writers. However, it is not restricted to existentialists. A contemporary and critical perspective is taken by Andrew Potter (2010), who gained a Ph.D in philosophy from the University of Toronto before becoming a journalist and author. His book examines why our search for authenticity in the modern world often, ironically, leads us to follow the next great 'fad'. Martin Seligman (2005),

Professor of Psychology at the University of Pennsylvania and former President of the American Psychological Association (APA), approaches the subject of authenticity from the perspective of positive psychology.

In order to be ourself, we need to know ourself

The principle of authenticity is closely aligned with self-knowledge. Anthony Hatzimoysis (2010) is Professor of Philosophy at the University of Athens. His book recognizes that self-knowledge has always been a central topic of philosophical inquiry, and he provides critical insight into the complexities of knowing one's self. That point alone is worth considering. It is hard to think of a major philosopher, from ancient times to the present, who refrained from pronouncing on the nature and the importance of self-knowledge. Self-knowledge has been a cornerstone of philosophy for centuries, therefore it must surely have significant importance to humanity. Maybe it is something that we ought to take seriously as a foundation of performance. John Corlett (1996) argues that self-knowledge be recognized and embraced by sport psychology. Mark Nesti (2004) goes on to argue that free will, responsibility, choice, authenticity and self-knowledge are all central to sport psychology theory and practice. His book provides a critical appraisal of existential approaches within sport psychology, and illustrates how they have been successfully applied within elite sport settings such as Premiership football.

In order to be authentic, we often have to transcend our ego

Our ego creates a façade. It attempts to present an image of us to the world, in the hope that the world will see us as the person we'd like to be. The work of Roy Baumeister

(Baumeister et al., 1993), Professor of Social Psychology at Florida State University, shows how threat to the ego, self-consciousness and self-presentation motivations negatively impact on performance. His work also shows the impact that expectations have in the creation of 'pressure'.

These concepts are also outlined by authors such as Abraham Tesser (Tesser, Wood and Stapel, 2005), Professor of Psychology at the University of Georgia. He developed the self-evaluation maintenance model and describes, from a social psychologist's perspective, how we build, defend and regulate our notions of self. Thomas Metzinger (2010) is an academic German philosopher whose book presents a view of the ego from both philosophy and neuroscience. He explains how the ego provides us with a view of ourself, which builds on his work on the study of consciousness.

Daniel Lapsley and Clark Power (1988), from Notre Dame University, provide a perspective on ego, self and identity from educational and developmental psychology. Andrew Sparkes (1998), Professor of Sport and Pedagogy at Liverpool John Moores University, and Rebecca Symes (2010), a practising Chartered Sport Psychologist, look at identity in an athletic context.

Of course, a journey into these realms inevitably leads to debates on the nature and existence of the self, consciousness and ego. I'm not going to engage in these debates. I'll leave you to read them yourself if you wish.

However, there are several practical guides on how to transcend our ego, start to know ourselves and be authentic. Some of these provide a guide on developing self-awareness. From an academic background, Kent Bach (1974) provides an insight into self-awareness, psychological insecurity, identity and alienation. Nathaniel Branden (2001), a psychotherapist with a Ph.D in philosophy, approaches self-awareness from the perspective of humanistic and positive psychology. By contrast, Mark Epstein's (1995) view of how to achieve self-awareness draws on his background as a classically trained Freudian psychotherapist who studied Buddhist methods. Therefore, he finds a good deal of common ground with Lama Tsultrim Allione (2008), an international Buddhist teacher. In contrast, Swaraj Wan (2009) presents experiential thoughts on how to know yourself and achieve more in your life.

Deeper self-knowledge is a topic covered by many of the existential authors. They would argue that self-knowledge is an aspiration – a journey that can never be fully completed. Therefore, it is the journey, and the development of ever greater self-knowledge, that is important, not the destination. The existential view of self-knowledge extends beyond self-awareness to an awareness of our patience, emotional responses and characteristics. Self-knowledge focuses on knowing who we are – our values, what we stand for and our deepest beliefs (Valle and Halling, 1989; Nesti, 2004).

Topic-specific approaches

The purpose of this book is to help you consistently achieve your peak performance. Peak performances, peak experiences, flow and the zone of optimal functioning are all well-researched areas within psychology and sport psychology. These themes are discussed in Chapter 1. Mihaly Csikszentmihalyi (1990) is the foremost researcher into the phenomena that constitute the *flow* state. His work examines states of peak performance and peak experience across a wide range of disciplines from a humanistic and positive psychology perspective. Susan Jackson, a sport psychology academic from the University of Queensland, joined forces with Csikszentmihalyi to apply the principles of *flow* to sports (Jackson and Csikszentmihalyi, 1999). In addition, researchers such as Yuri Hanin have also researched this area. Hanin developed the concept of the *Zone of Optimal Functioning*, which is reviewed by Dan Gould and Suzie Tuffey (1996). Many of the studies and accounts of peak performances report that performers enter a *mindless* state. Csikszentmihalyi (1990) actually describes flow as a state where we move beyond ourself and become unaware of ourself. Bob Rotella (2005), an applied sport psychologist who has worked with many of the world's top golfers, also advocates performing in the *mindless* state. In addition, researchers such as Kirstin Flegal and Michael Anderson (2008), from the University of Michigan, have researched the negative effect that over-thinking can have on expert performers. Their study examined the effects of over-thinking on golf putting performance in 80 golfers and found that performance decreased in experienced players when they were asked to analyze the skill before executing. Malcolm Gladwell (2005) describes how subconscious response is often better than planned or conscious response. This sentiment is echoed by coaches such as Tim Gallwey (1986) and Malcolm Cook (2005). Tim Gallwey advocates that we think less and he uses this concept as the basis of his Inner Game coaching methods. The Inner Game approach aims to help performers to 'just do it'. Gallwey identifies that in order to perform optimally we need to *trust* ourselves.

All these approaches share common ground. They suggest that we need to perform in a mindless state, so that we can 'just do it'. In order to do that, we need to take ourselves beyond any pre-occupation with ourself and our own thoughts. Being self-conscious, or concerned with self-presentation, interferes with performance (Baumeister et al., 1993). If we are to let go and trust ourself, we need to be ourself. In order to be ourself, we need to be happy with ourself. To be happy with ourself, we need to know ourself, which takes us back into our central themes of self-knowledge and authenticity.

The work of Gallwey and Csikszentmihalyi also identifies the importance of focusing on the most important cues in a performance. This is a key principle in Chapter 3. Recently, researchers such as Daniel Weissman (Weissman et al., 2006), Professor of Cognitive Perception at the University of Michigan, have identified that we can only focus on one thing at a time. His findings are supported by those of Adam Gazzaley, a neuroscientist from the University of California at Berkeley (Richtel, 2010). If we are focusing on our own thoughts, or our attention is taken up with concerns over how we will look or what people will think of us, our focus will not be fully honed on our performance. There are many who advocate that to hone focus we tune into our senses. Coaches such as Tim Gallwey (1986) and Malcolm Cook (2005) find common ground with Bob McKim, from Stanford University, who has extensively researched the field of human creativity. McKim states that 'seeing is encountering reality with all of your being. To encounter reality deeply, you cannot leave part of yourself behind. All of your senses, your emotions, your intellect, your language-making abilities – each contributes to seeing fully' (McKim, 1980: prelim i). All of this evidence supports the notion that we perform best when we have a simple, clear focus.

The subjects of focus, concentration and attention have been widely researched in psychology and sport psychology. Texts such as those by Thelma Horn (2008) and that by Jim Taylor and Greg Wilson (2005) provide overviews of the research and theoretical models. Taylor and Wilson (2005) provide an interesting insight into the topic, using perspectives from a researcher, a consultant sport psychologist, a coach and an athlete. Specific research on role clarity in sport is provided by Stuart Bray and Lawrence Brawley (2002a, 2002b), from the University of Waterloo. Csikszentmihalyi (1990) also identifies the importance of clear focus in performance outside of sport. The wider relationship between simplicity, clarity and performance is also covered by writers such as Paul Keller (2009) and Masaaki Imai (1986), who show that all three are central to effectiveness in business. Business strategist Jack Trout and communications consultant Steve Rivkin also highlight the importance of simplicity and clarity in business performance (Trout and Rivkin, 1998).

This evidence illustrates that having a simple, clear focus helps us to optimize our performance. Dana Lindsley from the US Air Force and colleagues from Pennsylvania State University have identified multi-level links between focus, confidence and increased performance (Lindsley et al., 1995). Their performance spiral models have been applied to sport by Thelma Horn (2008). These spirals, and the relationships between focus, confidence and motivation, are central topics in Chapter 2.

Additional support comes from the work of Albert Bandura (1997), Professor of Social Science and Psychology at Stanford University. He has developed a body of theory that recognizes the importance of *mastery* in the development of confidence. Bandura's theories of self-efficacy underpin many other theoretical models, such as Susan Harter's competence motivation theory and Robin Vealey's sport-specific model of self-confidence. Reviews of these models can be found in sport psychology texts such as that by Lavallee, Kremer, Moran and Williams (2004). Similar models have been applied to slightly different settings. Gary Dayton (2007), a clinical psychologist with a Ph.D from Rutgers University, applies a mindfulness–acceptance–commitment (MAC) model to enhancing performance in trading the stockmarket. The MAC model is an evolution of cognitive-behavioural therapy (CBT). Interestingly, the MAC model has been itself researched within sport by Gardner and Moore (2004).

Confidence is widely recognized as a key element in performance and is therefore the focus of Chapter 4. Kate

Hayes and her colleagues (2007) recognize that there are many factors that underpin confidence. Much of the sport psychology literature promotes the use of confidence building techniques, such as goal setting, self-talk, affirmations and imagery. Deborah Feltz's model of self-confidence suggests that confidence can be built on previous performance accomplishments, the vacarious confidence we might gain from others, verbal persuasion, imagined experiences and physiological states (Feltz, Short and Sullivan, 2008). However, those approaches are not included in the recommendations in Chapter 4 (or anywhere else in this book). It could be argued that the technique-based approaches used in much of sport psychology lead to manufactured confidence rather than to authentic confidence. Techniques such as verbal persuasion highlight that these approaches attempt to convince a person that they are confident. They try, in some way, to inject the person with confidence from an external source rather than cultivate it from within. Authors such as Valorie Burton (2007) and Larina Kase (2008) advocate the development of authentic confidence. This comes from knowing who you are (as opposed to focusing on what you do), giving yourself permission to be imperfect, dropping comparison with others and focusing on learning so that you fully develop your skills (Burton, 2007; Kase, 2008). Applied sport psychologists such as Terry Orlick (2000) also cite factors such as *preparedness* as keys to enhancing confidence and therefore performance. Orlick has studied the importance of preparedness in multiple disciplines, including sport and medicine.

Theoretical models such as achievement motivation illustrate the links between confidence and motivation. Andrew Elliot (Professor of Psychology from the University of Rochester) and his peer Carole Dweck (from Stanford University) provide an analysis of achievement motivation and establish the concept of 'competence' as an organizing framework (Elliot and Dweck, 2005). Motivation is a very well-studied area of psychology and is the focus of Chapter 5. Edward Deci and Richard Ryan (2002), from the University of Rochester, developed self-determination theory, a meta-theory comprising five mini theories, which provides a broad framework for the study of human motivation. James Shah (Professor of Neuroscience at Duke University) and Wendi Gardner (a social psychologist from Northwester University), provide a critical review of much of this motivational theory (Shah and Gardner, 2008).

Abraham Maslow also developed a theoretical model to explain human motivation. Maslow, a humanistic and developmental psychologist, was one of the first to study psychology from a positive perspective. Rather than researching neurotic behaviour and the negative side of mentality, he studied 'exemplary' people such as Albert Einstein. In a sense, he started to take psychology in a new direction. Although his 'hierarchy of needs' model has been criticized, it has been further expanded by many. Maslow's book, *Toward a Psychology of Being* (1998), started to develop his theories in the context of peak performance and peak experiences. Through this development, he also suggests that we need to move beyond ego in order to find peak experiences: a concept that he terms *self-transcendance*.

Specific research has been done on motivation and motives in the workplace by researchers such as James Linder (1998) and Mark Koltko-Rivera (2006). In addition, there is research and theoretical underpinning for the tools that are used in this book. Performance profiling is grounded in the theory of person-centred therapy, developed by George Kelly in 1955, and its effectiveness has been researched in multiple domains, including sport (Doyle and Parfitt, 2006).

In order to achieve peak performances consistently, we need to know what contributes to positive performance and

also what may detract from or interfere with our performance. Pressure is often cited as a phenomenon that can
negatively affect performance. My take on pressure, which
forms the basis of Chapter 6, is significantly different from
that of many researchers, academics and even many
applied practitioners in psychology. However, there is
support for the notion that if we experience pressure it is
because we have created it in our imagination. Sian
Beilock, Professor of Psychology at the University of
Chicago, suggests that it is our perception of stressful
situations that dictates our experience. Many of our existential friends would agree that we choose our lived
experiences. Beilock (2010) goes on to explain that even
when you construe a situation as threatening, you can
perform well. She draws together research from neuroscience and psychology, and shows that the body and mind
are inextricably linked.

Keith Markman is a Professor of Psychology at the
University of Ohio. He and his colleagues Julie Suhr and
William Klein of Princeton University (Markman et al.,
2008) integrate theory and research on imagination and
the generation of alternative realities. Their work
examines mental imagery, thought flow, narrative trans-
portation, fantasizing and counter-factual thinking. When
our experience of pressure is related to concerns over
future events, such experience is a projection from our
imagination. Therefore, these concepts and mechanisms
discussed by Markman and his colleagues provide strong
support for the notion that we generate pressure through
our imagination.

The reasons why we create this pressure have also been
the subject of research. In sport, John Dunn (1999), from
the University of Alberta, used a qualitative approach to
study the link between perfectionism and competitive
anxiety. Tal Ben-Shahar (2009), from the Department of
Psychology at Harvard University, sees that this phenom-

enon extends way beyond sport. He argues that the quest for perfection is not only fruitless but can also lead to unhappiness. Researchers have also drawn links between the uncertainty of outcomes and the perception of pressure. Work on the effect of *uncertainty* on performance can be seen by reading the work of Paul Boelen, from the Department of Clinical Health at the University of Utrecht (Boelen and Reijntjes, 2009).

In my work, I have often seen performers struggle when they are relying on their performance to inform their sense of self-worth. If the ego's need to generate positive self-image dominates our reason for performing, then we lose sight of the job at hand. Mark Fisher (1998) is a millionaire and author. Using golf as a vehicle, his fictional, semi-autobiographical account provides very practical advice on how to maintain a realistic view of the job at hand. His book helps to show how we often perceive a very simple job as a near-impossible feat. Martin Covington (1984), president and chair of psychology at the University of California at Berkeley, has studied the links between self-worth, fear of failure and reduced performance in education. Existentialists would suggest that if our ego is using our performance to inform our self-worth, it is because we do not have a strong knowledge of ourself or sufficient love for ourself. Victor Frankl (1959/1984) writes as a neurologist and psychiatrist who survived the Holocaust. From his experiences in the concentration camp, he argues that we find our reasons to live through finding meaning. Therefore, as humans, we look for meaning in our life experience. If our life is dominated by sport, or business, we develop an identity around that in order to help us find our meaning. However, Frankl, and many other existential writers, would suggest that genuine fulfilment requires deep self-knowledge and authenticity, rather than living out our labels. These issues are present throughout Chapters 6–9.

Our ultimate freedom and choice also dictate how much we test ourselves and push ourselves – whether we decide to live in our comfort zone or to explore our discomfort zones. Judith Bardwick (1995) recognizes the dangers of residing within the comfort zone. Judith Bardwick is a consultant business psychologist, a Fellow of the APA and a former Associate Dean at the University of Michigan. She has written a number of applied works on the psychology of corporate environments and organizational performance. In addition, Alistair White (2009), a management theorist who writes from a behavioural perspective, provides a framework for understanding the comfort zone and its impact on both performance and development. Other perspectives are provided by Mark Wolfinger and Ralph Heath. Wolfinger (2008) provides an applied perspective from the trading floor of the stockmarket. Heath (2009) helps to illustrate the importance of making mistakes, using his experiences as the founder of an advertising agency and a committed tri-athlete. He provides an insight into the way that businesses gain from mistakes (an almost inevitable consequence of operating in our discomfort zone), showing how they underpin confidence and innovation. Further views on creativity and innovation are provided by Robert Weisburg (2006), a cognitive psychologist from Temple University. He examines the creative processes behind Watson and Crick's modelling of DNA and Picasso's painting of Guernica as a basis. Perhaps the most poignant view is offered by existential writer Rollo May. He cites the importance of courage when stepping out of the comfort zone, taking risks and being creative (May, 1994).

Many of the concepts that have been discussed require us to push ourselves and experience stress. Initially, this may seem like an unfortunate consequence, but in reality it is actually something to be embraced. Hans Seyle (1975) was a pioneering researcher into the phenomena that we call stress. He described stress as the body's response to a challenge or demand. He dismisses the notion that challenging events are unhealthy – far from it. Seyle notes that 'eustress' (positive stress) is actually essential for health, describing it as 'the spice of life'. It is perhaps unusual therefore that eustress receives such little attention in psychological literature when compared with distress and anxiety (Le Ferve, Matheny and Kolt, 2003). It could be argued that our experiences of eustress, such as feelings of elation, are fundamental to living a fulfilled life. James Clash (2003), a writer for *Forbes* magazine, illustrates how this works in practice. His book, *Forbes to The Limits*, explores the mentality and experience that accompany feats of extreme human endeavour, such as mountaineering, polar exploration, lunar exploration, motor racing and even the development of the H-bomb.

The ability to push oneself and continually raise the bar is a feature of great performers. Geoff Colvin, senior editor at large for *Fortune* magazine, argues that World Class performances are the result of focused, deliberate practice. He provides evidence using a variety of research studies, particularly from sport and music. Colvin's arguments are influenced by the work of Anders Ericsson (Ericsson and Charness, 1999) and the models of sport expertise. The underlying proposition is that World Class performances are not a product of innate talent, but of hard work and practice. These sentiments are echoed in the autobiographies of successful self-made businessmen and entrepreneurs such as Duncan Bannatyne (2006), James Caan (2009) and Alan Sugar (2010). They are also supported by the biographical account of Warren Buffett's success, provided by Andrew Kilpatrick (2003).

All of this evidence presents us with a consistent message. Neither peak performance nor the strive for self-knowledge and authenticity can be accomplished at the click of a finger. They take time, application, dedication and often courage. Inevitably this will be uncomfortable. If we aspire to achieve our peak performance consistently, there may be some tough choices that we need to make. On the upside, your performance and success are ultimately within your control!

Bibliography

Allione, T. (2008) *Feeding the Demons: Ancient Wisdom for Resolving Inner Conflict*. London: Little, Brown & Co.

Anderson, M. (2000) *Doing Sport Psychology*. Champaign, IL: Human Kinetics.

Aristotle (trans. 1976) *The Nicomachean Ethics* ('Ethics'). Harmondsworth, UK: Penguin.

Aronoff, C.E. (2011) *Letting Go: Preparing Yourself to Relinquish Control of the Family Business*. Basingstoke, UK: Palgrave Macmillan.

Attwooll, J. (2008) Great Britain break world record in the team sprint cycling: Team GB have got their track cycling campaign in Beijng off to a flying start by breaking the world record in the team sprint qualification rounds. *Daily Telegraph*, 15 August 2008. Available at: http://www.telegraph.co.uk/sport/ other sports/ olympics/2562987/Britain-breaks-world-record-in-the-Team-Sprint-cycling-Beijing-Olympics-2008.html (accessed 15 December 2010).

Australian Institute of Sport (2010) *Self Confidence: Athlete Tipsheet*. Canberra: Australian Institute of Sport.

Ayers, W. (2001) *To Teach: The Journey of a Teacher*. New York: Teachers College Press.

Bach, K. (1974) *Exit Existentialism: A Philosophy of Self-Awareness*. Flourence, KY: Wadsworth Publishing.

Bandura, A. (1997) *Self-Efficacy: The Exercise of Control*. New York: Worth Publishers.

Bannatyne, D. (2006) *Anyone Can Do It: My Story*. London: Orion.

Bardwick, J. (1995). *Danger in the Comfort Zone: How to Break the Entitlement Habit that's Killing American Business*. New York: American Management Association.

Baumeister, R.F., Hamilton, J.C. and Tice, D.M. (1985) Public versus private expectancy of success: Confidence booster or performance pressure? *Journal of Personality and Social Psychology, 48*(6), 1447–1457.

Baumeister, R.F., Heatherton, T.F. and Tice, D.M. (1993) When ego threats lead to self-regulation failure: Negative consequences of high self-esteem. *Journal of Personality and Social Psychology, 64*(1), 141–156.

Baumeister, R.F. and Showers, C.J. (1986) A review of paradoxical performance effects: Choking under pressure in sports and mental tests. *European Journal of Social Psychology, 16*(4), 361–383.

Beilock, S. (2010) *Choke*. New York: Free Press.

Benjamin, H. (1989) *Basic Self-Knowledge*. New York: Red Wheel.

Ben-Shahar, T. (2009) *The Pursuit of Perfect: How to Stop Chasing Perfection and Start Living a Richer, Happier Life*. New York: McGraw-Hill Professional.

Berkow, I. (1984) Beaman's moment suspended in time. *New York Biographical Service, 15*, 289–290.

Blanke, G. (2007) How to stop overthinking your life and start living. *Real Simple*, August 2007.

Boelen, P. A. and Reijntjes, A. (2009) Intolerance of uncertainty and social anxiety. *Journal of Anxiety Disorders, 23*, 130–135

Branden, N. (1984) *Honoring the Self*. London: Bantam Press.

Branden, N. (2001) *The Psychology of Self-Esteem: A Revolutionary Approach to Self-Understanding that Launched a New Era in Modern Psychology*. New York: Jossey-Bass.

Bray, S.R. and Brawley, L.R. (2002a) Role efficacy, role clarity and role performance effectiveness. *Small Group Research, 33*(2), 233–253

Bray, S.R. and Brawley, L.R. (2002b) Efficacy for independent role functions: Evidence from the sport domain. *Small Group Research, 33*(6), 644–666.

Brown, T. (2008) Tim Brown on creativity and play. Keynote presentation to Technology Education Design Conference, 5 November 2008. Available at: http://www.ted.com/talks/tim_brown_on_creativity_and_play.html (accessed 31 March 2011).

Bull, S.J. (1996) *The Mental Game Plan: Getting Psyched for Sport*. London: Sport Dynamics.

Burton, A. (1963) The authentic person in existential psychology. *Pastoral Psychology, 20*(3), 17–26.

Burton, V. (2007) *Why Not You?* Colorado Springs, CO: WaterBrook Press.

Caan, J. (2009) *The Real Deal: My Story from Brick Lane to Dragon's Den.* London: Virgin.

Caine, R.N. and Caine, G. (1990) Understanding a brain-based approach to learning and teaching. *Educational Leadership,* 48(2), 66–70.

Chopra, D., Williamson, M. and Ford, D. (2010) *The Shadow Effect: Illuminating the Hidden Power of Your True Self.* New York: HarperOne.

Christenson, M. (2010) World Cup 2010: Capello says pressure hindered England players. *The Guardian,* 21 June 2010. Available at: http://www.guardian.co.uk/football/2010/jun/21/world-cup-fabio-capello-pressure-england (accessed 8 August 2011).

Clash, M.J. (2003) *Forbes to the Limits: Pushing Yourself to the Edge in Adventure and in Business.* New York: Wiley.

Collins, J.C. (2001) *Good to Great: Why Some Companies Make the Leap and Others Don't.* New York: Harper Business.

Colvin, G. (2008) *Talent is Overrated: What Really Separates World Class Performers from Everybody Else.* New York: Portfolio.

Cook, M. (2005) *The FreeFlow Method.* Morpeth, UK: Sports-Coach21.

Cork, A., Justham, L. and West, A. (2008) Cricket batting: Stroke timing of a batsman when facing a bowler and a bowling machine. *The Engineering of Sport, 7,* 143–150.

Corlett, J. (1996) Sophistry, Socrates and sport psychology. *The Sport Psychologist, 10*(1), 84–94.

Cotterill, S. and Johnson, P. (2008) *Exploring the Concept of the Comfort Zone in Professional Soccer Players.* Association for Applied Sport Psychology Annual Conference, September 2008, St Louis, MO.

Covey, S.R. (2004) *The 7 Habits of Highly Effective People.* New York: Simon & Schuster.

Covington, M.V. (1984) The self-worth theory of achievement motivation: Findings and implications. *Elementary School Journal, 85*(1), 5–20.

Covington, M.V. (1992) *Making the Grade: A Self Worth Perspective on Motivation and School Reform.* Cambridge, UK: Cambridge University Press.

Crust, L. and Nesti, M.S. (2006) A review of psychological momentum in sports: Why qualitative research is needed. *Athletic Insights, 8*(1), 1–15.

Csikszentmihalyi, M. (1990) *Flow: The Psychology of Optimal Experience*. New York: Harper & Row.

Csikszentmihalyi, M. (2008) *Creativity, fulfillment and flow*. Keynote presentation to Technology Education Design Conference, 24 October 2008. Available at: http://www.youtube.com/watch?v=fXIeFJCqsPs (accessed 15 December 2010).

Damasio, A.R. (2010) *Self Comes to Mind: Constructing the Conscious Brain*. Great Haven, MI: Brilliance Corporation.

Davison, R.C. and Williams, A.M. (2009) The use of sports science in preparation for Olympic competition. *Journal of Sports Sciences*, 27(13), 1363–1365.

Day, M.C., Thatcher, J., Greenlees, I. and Woods, B. (2006) The causes of and psychological responses to Lost Move Syndrome in national level trampolinists. *Journal of Applied Sport Psychology*, 18, 151–166.

Dayton, G. (2007) Trading psychology – the universal law of trading confidence. *Trading Psychology Edge*, September 2007. Available at: http://ezinearticles.com/?expert-Gary_Dayton, Psy.D. (accessed 8 August 2011).

Deci, E.L. and Ryan, R.M. (1985) *Intrinsic Motivation and Self-Determination in Human Behavior*. New York: Plenum Press.

Deci, E.L. and Ryan, R.M. (2002) *Handbook of Self-Determination Research*. Rochester, NY: University of Rochester Press.

Deci, E.L., Ryan, R.M. and Koestner, R. (1999) A meta-analytic review of experiments examining the effects of extrinsic rewards on intrinsic motivation. *Psychological Bulletin*, 125(6), 627–668.

Decker, K.S. and Eberl, J.T. (2005) *Star Wars and Philosophy: More Powerful Than You Can Possibly Imagine*. Peru, IL: Carus Publishing.

Dilman, I. (1999) *Free Will*, London: Routledge.

Donnelly, J.H. and Ivancevich, J.M. (1975) Role clarity and the salesman. *Journal of Marketing*, 39(1), 71–74.

Douglas, M. (2000) *The Disciplined Trader: Developing Winning Attitudes*. Englewood Cliffs, NJ: Prentice-Hall.

Doyle, J. and Parfitt, G. (2006) Performance profiling and predictive validity. *Journal of Applied Sport Psychology*, 8(2), 160–170.

Dunkel, S.E. (1989) *The Audition Process: Anxiety Management and Coping Strategies*. Hillside, NY: Pendragon Press.

Dunn, J.G.H. (1999) A theoretical framework for structuring the content of competitive worry in ice hockey. *Journal of Sport and Exercise Psychology*, 21, 259–278.

Dunn, J.G.H. and Syrotuik, D.G. (2003) An investigation of multidimensional worry dispositions in high contact sport. *Psychology of Sport and Exercise, 4*, 265–282.

Elliot, A. and Dweck, C.S. (2005) *Handbook of Competence and Motivation.* New York: Guilford Press.

England & Wales Cricket Board (2005) *Planning for Long Term Success.* London: England & Wales Cricket Board.

Epstein, J. (2006) *The Little Book on Big Ego: A Guide to Manage and Control the Egomaniacs in Your Life.* New York: Alnola Productions.

Epstein, M. (1995) *Thoughts Without A Thinker: Psychotherapy from a Buddhist Perspective.* New York: Basic Books.

Ericsson, K.A. and Charness, N. (1994) Expert performance: Its structure and acquisition. *American Psychologist, 49*, 725–747.

Ericsson, K.A. and Charness, N. (1999) Becoming and export – training or talent? In Ceci, S.J. and Williams, W.M. (Eds.), *The Nature–Nurture Debate: The Essential Readings* (pp. 200–205). Malden, MA: Blackwell.

Farrow, D., Baker, J. and MacMahon, C. (2007) *Developing Sport Expertise: Researchers and Coaches Put Theory into Practice.* London: Routledge.

Feltz, D.L., Short, S.E. and Sullivan, P.J. (2008) *Self-Efficacy in Sport: Research Strategies for Work with Athletes, Teams and Coaches.* Champaign, IL: Human Kinetics.

Fisher, M. (1998) *The Golfer and the Millionaire.* New York: Cassell Illustrated.

Flegal, K. and Anderson, M. (2008) Overthinking skilled motor performance. *Psychonomic Bulletin and Review, 15*, 927–932.

Frankl, V.E. (1984) *Man's Search for Meaning.* New York: Touchstone. (Original work published 1959.)

Gallwey, T. (1986) *The Inner Game of Tennis.* London: Pan Books.

Gallwey, T. (2003) *The Inner Game of Work.* New York: Texere Publishing.

Gardner, F.L. and Moore, Z.E. (2004) A mindfulness–acceptance–commitment-based approach to athletic performance enhancement: Theoretical considerations. *Behavior Therapy, 35*, 707–723.

Gerrard, S. (2010) England skipper Steven Gerrard tells under-fire stars to make their nation proud ahead of do-or-die showdown with Slovenia. *Daily Record*, 23 June 2010. Available at: http://www.dailyrecord.co.uk/football/world-cup-2010/news/2010/06/23/england-skipper-steven-gerrard-tells-under-fire-

stars-to-make-their-nation-proud-ahead-of-do-or-die-show
down-with-slovenia-86908-22353116/ (accessed 15 December
2010).

Gilbert, J. (2005) Self knowledge is the pre-requisite of humanity:
Personal development and self-awareness in aid workers.
Development in Practice, 15(1), 64–69.

Gilson, C., Pratt, M., Roberts, K. and Weymes, E. (2000) *Peak
Performance: Business Lessons from the World's Top Sports
Organisations*. New York: Harper Collins Business.

Gladwell, M. (2005) *Blink: The Power of Thinking Without
Thinking*. New York: Allen Lane.

Gladwell, M. (2008) *Outliers: The Story of Success*. London:
Little, Brown & Co.

Glasser, W. (1999) *Choice Theory: A New Psychology of Personal
Freedom*. New York: HarperCollins.

Gonzalez, J. (2008) 0.27 seconds: All that separates Michael
Phelps and Ryan Lochte. *Men's Journal*, 16 July 2008. Avail-
able at: http://www.mensjournal.com/027-seconds (accessed 8
August 2011).

Gould, D. and Tuffey, S. (1996) Zones of Optimal Functioning: A
review and critique. *Anxiety, Stress and Coping, 9*(1), 53–68.

Graue, B. (2006) The transformational power of reviewing.
Education Researcher, 35(8), 36–41.

Grove, J.R., Lavallee, D. and Gordon, S. (1997) Coping with
retirement from sport: The influence of athletic identity.
Journal of Applied Sport Psychology, 9, 191–203.

Halden-Brown, S. (2003) *Mistakes Worth Making: How to Turn
Sports Errors into Athletic Excellence*. Champaign, IL: Human
Kinetics.

Hamilton, J. (2008) Think you're multi-tasking? Think again.
NRP, 2 October 2008. Available at: http://www.npr.org/
templates/story/story.php?storyId=95256794   (accessed   8
August 2011).

Hardcastle, P. (2008) *Psychology of Motorsport Success: How to
Improve Your Performance with Mental Skills Training*.
Sparkford, UK: J.H. Haynes & Co.

Harlow, J. (1999) Fear drives actors from the stage. *The Sunday
Times*, 14 February 1999, p. 13.

Harris, N. (2009) In the Pool: Team GB can make a bigger splash
in 2012. *The Independent*, 18 March 2009. Available at: http://
www.independent.co.uk/sport/general/others/in-the-pool-team-
gb-can-make-a-bigger-splash-in-2012-1647188.html (accessed 8
August 2011).

Hartley, S.R. (2007) Are you thinking what your athlete is thinking? *Coaching Edge*, *8*, 20–21.

Hartley, S.R. (2010a) Controlling your confidence. *Squash Player*, *38*(1), 15.

Hartley, S.R. (2010b) No such thing as pressure. *Squash Player*, *38*(2), 19.

Hartley, S.R. (2010c) Real goals. *Squash Player*, *38*(3), 17.

Hartley, S.R. (2010d) Motivation: The driving force. *Squash Player*, *38*(4), 22.

Hartley, S.R. (2010e) Learn from everything. *Squash Player*, *38*(6), 24.

Hartley, S.R. (2010f) Athletic focus & sport psychology: Key to peak performance. *Podium Sports Journal*, December 2010. Available at: http://www.podiumsportsjournal.com/2010/12/09/athletic-focus-sport-psychology-key-to-peak-performance/ (accessed 21 December 2010).

Hartley, S.R. (2010g) Momentum shifts in sport: Value the psychology behind them. *Podium Sports Journal*, December 2010. Available at: http://www.podiumsportsjournal.com/2010/12/22/momentum-shifts-in-sports-value-the-psychology-behind-them/ (accessed 4 April 2011).

Hartley, S.R. (2011) Maintaining momentum. *Squash Player*, *39*(2), 28–29.

Hartley, S.R. and Laver, D.J. (2011) *Street Soccer Coaching*. Yeovil, UK: International Street Soccer Association.

Hatzimoysis, A. (2010) *Self-Knowledge*. New York: Oxford University Press.

Hayes, K., Maynard, I., Thomas, O. and Bawden, M. (2007) Sources of confidence identified by World Class sport performers. *Journal of Applied Sport Psychology*, *19*(4), 434–456.

Heath, R. (2009) *Celebrating Failure: The Power of Taking Risks, Making Mistakes and Thinking Big*. Pompton Plains, NJ: Career Press.

Horn, T. (2008) *Advances in Sport Psychology*. Champaign, IL: Human Kinetics.

Huw, J. (2010) Rugby World Cup 2011. Are the All Blacks peaking too soon? *Suite101.com*, 2 August 2010. Available at: http://www.suite101.com/content/rugby-world-cup-2011–are-the-all-blacks-peaking-too-soon–a268927 (accessed 15 December 2010).

Imai, M. (1986) *Kaizen: The Key To Japan's Competitive Success*. London: McGraw-Hill.

Jackson, S. and Csikszentmihalyi, M. (1999) *Flow in Sports*. Champaign, IL: Human Kinetics.

Jauncey, P. (2002) *Managing Yourself & Others*. Brisbane: CopyRight Publishing.

Johnson, M. (1996) *Slaying the Dragon: How to Turn Your Small Steps into Great Feats*. New York: HarperCollins.

Johnson, P. and Cotterill, S. (2008) Towards an understanding of player comfort zones: Clarifying perceptions and awareness. Science and Soccer Conference, 15–16 May 2008, Liverpool, UK.

Jones, G. and Moorhouse, A. (2007) *Developing Mental Toughness*. London: How to Books.

Jones, G., Hanton, S. and Connaughton, D. (2007) A framework for mental toughness in the world's best performers. *The Sport Psychologist, 21*, 243–264.

Jowett, S. and Lavallee, D. (2007) *Social Psychology in Sport*. Champaign, IL: Human Kinetics.

Jung, C.G. (1968) *Collected Works of C. G. Jung* (Vol. 9, Part 1, 2nd ed.). New York: Princeton University Press.

Kase, L. (2008) *The Confident Leader*. New York: McGraw-Hill.

Kekes, J. (1995) *Moral Wisdom and Good Lives*. Ithaca, NY: Cornell University Press.

Keller, P. (2009) *The Six Sigma Handbook*. London. McGraw-Hill Professional.

Key, A. (2006) Knowing your role in rugby. *Rugby Football Union Technical Journal*, pp. 1–6.

Kilpatrick, A. (2003) *Of Permanent Value: The Story of Warren Buffett*. New York: APKE.

Kloosterman, P. (1988) Self confidence and motivation in mathematics. *Journal of Educational Psychology, 80*(3), 345–351.

Koestenbaum, P. and Block, P. (2001) *Freedom and Accountability at Work: Applying Philosophic Insight to the Real World*. New York: Jossey-Bass.

Koltko-Rivera, M.E. (2006) Rediscovering the later version of Maslow's Hierarchy of Needs: Self-transcendence and opportunities for theory, research and unification. *Review of General Psychology, 10*(4), 302–317.

Lane, A. (2001) Relationship between perceptions of performance expectations and mood amongst distance runners. *Journal of Science and Medicine in Sport, 4*(1), 116–128.

Lapsley, D.K. and Power, F.C. (1988) *Self, Ego, and Identity: Integrative Approaches*. New York: Springer.

Lavallee, D., Kremer, J., Moran, A. and Williams, M. (2004)

Sports Psychology: Contemporary Themes. New York: Palgrave Macmillan.

Le Ferve, M., Matheny, J. and Kolt, G.S. (2003) Eustress, distress, and interpretation in occupational stress. *Journal of Managerial Psychology*, *18*(7), 726–744.

Lieberman, J.N. (1977) *Playfulness: Its Relationship to Imagination and Creativity*. New York: Academic Press.

Linder, J.R. (1998) Understanding Employee Motivation. *Journal of Extension*, *36*(3), 1–8.

Lindsley, D.H., Brass, D.J. and Thomas, J.B. (1995) Efficacy–performance spirals: A multilevel perspective. *Academy of Management Review*, *20*(3), 645–678.

Luciani, J.J. (2004) *The Power of Self-Coaching: The 5 Essential Steps to Creating the Life You Want*. New York: Wiley.

Manz, C.C. (2000) *Emotional Discipline: The Power to Choose How You Feel*. San Francisco: Berrett-Koehler.

Manz, C.C. (2002) *The Power of Failure*. San Francisco: Berrett-Koehler.

Markman, K.D., Klein, W.M.P. and Suhr, J.A. (2008) *Handbook of Imagination and Mental Simulation*. Hove, UK: Psychology Press.

Martin Fischer, J. and Ravizza, M. (1998) *Responsibility and Control: A Theory of Moral Responsibility*. Cambridge, UK: Cambridge University Press.

Maslow, A. (1970) *Motivation and Personality* (3rd ed.). New York: Harper Row.

Maslow, A. (1998) *Toward a Psychology of Being* (3rd ed.). New York: John Wiley.

May, R. (1953) *Man's Search For Himself*. New York: W.W. Norton & Co.

May, R. (1994) *The Courage to Create*. New York: W.W. Norton & Co.

McDonald, J., Orlick, T. and Letts, M. (1995) Mental readiness in surgeons and its links to performance excellence in surgery. *Journal of Pediatric Orthopedics*, *15*(5), 691–697.

McKim, R. (1980) *Experiences in Visual Thinking* (2nd ed.). California: Brooks/Cole Publishing.

Metzinger, T. (2010) *The Ego Tunnel: The Science of the Mind and the Myth of the Self*. New York: Basic Books.

Midgley, N. and Abrams, M.S. (1974) Fear of success and locus of control in young women. *Journal of Consulting and Clinical Psychology*, *42*(5), 737.

Miller, J.R. (1994) Fear of success: Psychodynamic implications. *Journal of American Academy of Psychoanalysis, 22*, 129–136.

Moller, A.C., Deci, E.L. and Ryan, R.M. (2006) Choice and ego-depletion: The moderating role of autonomy. *Personality and Social Psychology Bulletin, 32*(8), 1024–1036.

Murphy, S. (1996) *The Achievement Zone*. New York: Berkeley.

Najemy, R. (2002) *The Psychology of Happiness*. New York: Holistic Harmony.

Nesti, M.S. (2004) *Existential Psychology and Sport: Theory and Application*. Oxford, UK: Routledge.

Nideffer, R.M. (2007) Reliability and validity of the Attentional and Interpersonal Style Inventory (TAIS) concentration scales. In Smith, D. and Bar-Eli, M. (Eds.), *Essential Readings in Sport and Exercise Psychology* (pp. 265–277), Champaign, IL: Human Kinetics.

Orlick, T. (1998) *Embracing Your Potential*. Champaign, IL: Human Kinetics.

Orlick, T. (2000) *In Pursuit of Excellence: How to Win in Sport and Life Through Mental Training* (3rd ed.). Champaign, IL: Human Kinetics.

Pijpers, J.R., Oudejans, R.R.D., Holsheimer, F. and Bakker, F.C. (2003) Anxiety–performance relationships in climbing: A process oriented approach. *Psychology of Sport and Exercise, 4*, 283–304.

Potter, A. (2010) *The Authenticity Hoax: How We Get Lost Finding Ourselves*. New York: Harper.

Pureakero, P.R. (2008) *Commenting on Csikszentmihalyi, M. (2008) Creativity, fulfillment and flow*. Keynote presentation to Technology Education Design Conference, 24 October 2008. Available at: http://www.youtube.com/watch?v=fXIeFJCqsPs (accessed 15 December 2010).

Rabideau, S.T. (2005) Effects of achievement motivation on behaviour. *Personality Research*, November 2005. Available at: http://www.personalityresearch.org/papers/rabideau.html (accessed 8 August 2011).

Rauch, S. (2010) Trager®: A body/mind approach in sport psychology. *Podium Sports Journal*, 1 April 2010. Available at: http://www.podiumsportsjournal.com/2010/04/01/trager%C2%AE-a-bodymind-approach-in-sports-psychology/ (accessed 15 December 2010).

Ravizza, K. (1984) Qualities of the peak experience. In Silva, J.M. and Weinberg, R.S. (Eds.), *Psychological Foundations of Sport* (pp. 452–461). Champaign, IL: Human Kinetics.

Reitman, E.E. and Williams, C.D. (1961) Relationships between hope of success and fear of failure, anxiety, and need for achievement. *Journal of Abnormal and Social Psychology, 62*(2), 465–467.

Richtel, M. (2010) Multitasking hurts brain's ability to focus, scientists say. *Seattle Times*, 6 June 2010. Available at: http://www.seattletimes.nwsource.com/html/nationworld/2012049123_web multitask07.html (accessed 8 August 2011).

Robinson, K. (2006) *Do schools kill creativity?* Keynote presentation to Technology Education Design Conference, 26 June 2006. Available at: http://www.ted.com/talks/ken_robinson_says_schools_kill_creativity.html (accessed 15 December 2010).

Robinson, K. (2010) *Bring on the learning revolution.* Keynote presentation to Technology Education Design Conference, 24 May 2010. Available at: http://www.ted.com/talks/sir_ken_robinson_bring_on_the_revolution.html (accessed 15 December 2010).

Rotella, R.J. (2004) *The Golfer's Mind.* New York: Free Press.

Rotella, R.J. (2005) *Putting Out Of Your Mind.* London: Pocket Books.

Sadd, S., Lenauer, M., Shaver, P. and Dunivant, N. (1978) Objective measurement of fear of success and fear of failure: A factor analytic approach. *Journal of Consulting and Clinical Psychology, 46*(3), 405–416.

Schwartz, B. (2000) Self-determination: The tyranny of freedom. *American Psychologist, 55*, 79–88.

Schwartz, B. (2002) *Choice and Well-Being: Why Less Can Be More.* Paper presented at First European Conference on Positive Psychology, Winchester, UK, 28–30 June 2002.

Seaward, B.L. (2006) *Managing Stress: Principles and Strategies for Health and Wellbeing.* Sudbury, MA: Jones & Bartlett Publishing.

Seligman, M.E.P. (2005) *Authentic Happiness: Using the New Positive Psychology to Realize Your Potential for Lasting Fulfillment.* New York: Free Press.

Seyle, H. (1975) *Stress Without Distress.* New York: New American Library.

Shah, J.Y. and Gardner, W.L. (2008) *Handbook of Motivation Science.* New York: Guilford Press.

Sommers-Flanagan, J. and Sommers-Flanagan, R. (2004) Existential theory and therapy. In Sommers-Flanagan, J. and Sommers-Flanagan, R. (Eds.), *Counseling and Psychotherapy*

Theories in Context and Practice: Skills, Strategies and Techniques (pp. 138–173). New York: John Wiley.

Sorensen, C.W. (1994) Success and education in South Korea. *Comparative Education Review*, *38*(1), 10–35.

Sparkes, A.C. (1998) Athletic identity: An Achilles' heel to the survival of self. *Qualitative Health Research*, *8*(5), 644–664.

Spinelli, E. (1996) The existential–phenomenological paradigm. In Woolfe, R. and Dryden, W. (Eds.), *Handbook of Counselling Psychology* (pp. 180–200). London: Sage.

Starkes, J.L. and Ericsson, K.A. (2003) *Expert Performance in Sports: Advances in Research on Sport Expertise*. Champaign, IL: Human Kinetics.

Sugar, A. (2010) *What You See Is What You Get: My Autobiography*. London: Macmillan.

Sutcliffe, P. (1997) Out of tune with the rest of us. *The Sunday Times*, 8 June 2007, p. 6 (Supplement: Stress Manager, Part 4: Raising Your Game).

Symes, R. (2010) Understanding athletic identity: 'Who am I?'. *Podium Sports Journal*, 24 May 2010. Available at: http://www. podiumsportsjournal.com/2010/05/24/understanding-athletic-identity-who-am-i/ (accessed 15 December 2010).

Taylor, J. (2010) Understanding focus in sports. *Psychology Today*, 13 July 2010. Available at: http://www.psychologytoday. com/blog/the-power-prime/201007/sports-understanding-focus-in-sports (accessed 15 December 2010).

Taylor, J. and Wilson, G.S. (2005) *Applying Sport Psychology: Four Perspectives*. Champaign, IL: Human Kinetics.

Tenenbaum, G. and Eklund, R.C. (2007) *Handbook of Sport Psychology*. New York: Wiley.

Tesser, A., Wood, J.V. and Stapel, D.A. (2005) *On Building, Defending and Regulating the Self: A Psychological Perspective*. New York: Psychology Press.

Times 100 (2010) Siemens: Motivation within a creative environment. *The Times 100 Business Case Study*. Available at: http://www.thetimes100.co.uk/downloads/siemens/siemens_ 15_full.pdf (accessed 15 December 2010).

Torres, D. and Weil, E. (2009) *Age is Just a Number: Achieve Your Dreams at Any Age in Your Life*. New York: Crown Archetypes.

Trimble, V. (1993) *Overnight Success: FedEx and Frederick Smith, Its Renegade Creator*. New York: Crown.

Trout, J. and Rivkin, S. (1998) *The Power of Simplicity*. New York: McGraw-Hill.

Vaillant, G.E. (1992) *Ego Mechanisms of Defence*. Washington, DC: American Psychiatric Press.

Vajda, P.D. (2008) *Why Being Authentic is So Difficult*. Atlanta, GA: Spirit Heart.

Valle, R. and Halling, S. (1989) *Existential–Phenomenological Perspectives in Psychology: Exploring the Breadth of Human Experience*. New York: Plenum Press.

Verbeke, W. and Bagozzi, R.P. (2000) Sales call anxiety: Exploring what it means when fear rules a sales encounter. *Journal of Marketing*, *64*(3), 88–101.

Wan, S. (2009) *Knowledge of Self: Impossible is Nothing*. Charleston, SC: CreateSpace.

Weinberg, R.S. and Gould, D. (2010) *Foundations of Sport and Exercise Psychology*. Champaign, IL: Human Kinetics.

Weisberg, R. (2006) *Creativity: Understanding Innovation in Problem Solving, Science, Invention, and the Arts*. New York: Wiley.

Weissman, D.H., Roberts, K.C., Visscher, K.M. and Woldorff, M.G. (2006) The neural bases of momentary lapses in attention. *Nature Neuroscience*, *9*, 971–978.

White, A.A.K. (2009) *From Comfort Zone to Performance Management*. New York: White & MacLean Publishing.

Wilkinson, J. (2008) *Tackling Life: Striving for Perfection*. London: Headline.

Wolfinger, M.D. (2008) *The Rookies Guide to Options: The Beginner's Handbook of Trading Equity Options*. Cedar Falls, IA: W&A Publishing.

Yalom, I.D. (1980) *Existential Psychotherapy*. New York: Basic Books.

Young, J.A. and Pain, M.D. (1999) The zone: Evidence of a universal phenomenon for athletes across sports. *Athletic Insight*, *1*(3), 21–30.

Zander, R.S. and Zander, B. (2000) *The Art of Possibility: Transforming Professional and Personal Life*. Harvard, MA: Harvard Business School Press.

Zanna, M.P. (2009) *Advances in Experimental Social Psychology*, *Vol. 41*. New York: Academic Press.

Zeidner, M. (1998) *Test Anxiety: The State of the Art*. New York: Plenum Press.

Index